A DADS REVOLUTION

"Homesickness is one of our society's deepest diseases, and fatherlessness rests at its core. This book describes a compelling and effective cure. With candid honesty about the costs of fatherlessness in his own life, and even the costs of his own failures as a father, Marvin powerfully portrays a journey of healing and redemption. In so doing, this book is an invitation and a loud call to action.

The book sets out a clear regimen for the healing of fatherlessness in individuals' lives and in our society. The path through the ravages of fear, shame, and self-loathing that fuel this disease is both simple and hard: vulnerable honesty, teachable humility, and committed community. With powerful testimonies from his own life, and from dozens of other men, Marvin opens up an invitation to a better way than the emotional detachment, toxic masculinity, and self-indulging escapism that can characterize lives infected with the disease of fatherlessness.

Wise gems refined through the fires of failure and faithful work to rebuild broken hearts and families fill this book. It is a book of wisdom, not the knowledge gained through academic degrees, but the insights gained through the school of suffering. Often our society reacts only to the symptoms of the disease, responding with judgment, rejection, and even incarceration. This book speaks to the causes and demonstrates the effectiveness of very practical steps toward healing.

As a result, this book robs us of our excuses for remaining unengaged, and calls us all to take action. This is an invitation to join in committed communities that surround men for whom their life experience and our society's systems have robbed them of fatherhood. Together, in helping men know the dignity and worth that comes through the love of our Heavenly Father, a love made tangible in our empathy and persistence, healing is at hand, and men, their families, and our broader society will flourish."

Tim Dearborn, PhD
Retired Pastor and Former Director of
the Lloyd John Ogilvie Institute of Preaching
at Fuller Theological Seminary, Author of 15
books including *Christ's Heart Our Home*, *The Short-Term Missions Workbook*, and *Beyond Duty: A Passion for Christ, a Heart for Mission*

"Marvin gives a profound message for all dads, not just those coming out of crisis and trauma. Being present, being an encourager, being a champion—all kids deserve the kind of dad Marvin describes. I celebrate the work that Marvin himself has put in and his obedience to the Lord's calling to pass it forward."

Melissa Gehrig
Executive Director Emeritus, Vision House
DADS and C3Leaders Board of Directors

"For too long our society has either ignored or been indifferent to the terrible consequences of growing up without a father. Fatherless boys are more likely to abuse drugs and alcohol, commit crimes, drop out of school, and engage in other self-destructive behavior. Moreover, the effects of fatherlessness extend well beyond the child and their father. The harm extends to entire families and is multigenerational. While the societal costs of fatherlessness are devastating, on a personal level, they are heartbreaking.

You cannot read these pages without being moved and inspired to take action. Whether you were raised without a father, need to reestablish a relationship with your own children, or just want to make a difference in your community, this book is for you. This is the kind of revolution we need. Pass it on."

Joseph G. Marra
Attorney, Seattle, WA

"Marvin Charles writes with a voice that is honest, humble, and hopeful. His story offers a profound understanding of the power of listening, and of the importance of creating safe spaces for grief and emotional pain to be shared. He shows us that community can foster healing—and that 'if we truly want to change the trajectory of fatherhood, of families, of entire generations, we have to do it together.' This book invites readers on a powerful journey of understanding this truth."

Karen Johnson
Senior Associate, Centered

"Congratulations to my good friend Marvin for his latest book, *A Dad's Revolution*. I was able to hear his gentle voice speaking throughout. He does not give us the 'how tos' that we are accustomed to read in books for fathers. He has emerged from his nightmare of fatherlessness to a new and hopeful day of 'grandfatherhood.' By sharing his own story and admitting he still has a long way to go, he encourages other fathers who are "in the trenches" and may feel like giving up.

He and Jeanett have been a team throughout the journey. As they have walked this out, they have left a well-marked pathway for men and their families to follow. Marvin 'puts the cookies on the lower shelf,' in this very accessible book. The biblically based principles he has discovered work for men from all ethnic, socio-economic, and religious backgrounds. This powerful little book will add to his ongoing legacy of giving hope to fathers…one father and one family at a time."

Jamie Bohnett
Author and Lay Pastor

"This book will awaken the reader to the unseen pain, the need for a change, and the challenges before us if we want to stop the continuing cycle of violence and prison in our world today. Through his personal stories and those of clients he has helped, Marvin shows how father loss has devastated our society and how the response of DADS is changing the future for thousands of children through a restored connection to their fathers. By demonstrating how change occurs, he shows others how to do the same. *A DADS Revolution* will inspire the reader to a place of understanding and action."

Greg Towery
Men's Ministry Leader,
Divine Alternatives for Dads Services

A DADS REVOLUTION

Pass It On

Marvin Charles

A DADS Revolution: Pass It On
First Edition Trade Book, 2025
Copyright © 2025 by Marvin Charles

All rights reserved. No part of this publication may be reproduced, stored in a retrieval system, or transmitted in any form by any means—electronic, mechanical, photocopy, recording, or otherwise—except for brief quotations in critical reviews or articles, without the prior permission of the publisher, except as provided by U.S. copyright law.

Scriptures taken from the Holy Bible, New International Version®, NIV®. Copyright © 1973, 1978, 1984, 2011 by Biblica, Inc.™ Used by permission of Zondervan. All rights reserved worldwide. www.zondervan.com The "NIV" and "New International Version" are trademarks registered in the United States Patent and Trademark Office by Biblica, Inc.®

Note: The names of some of the individuals in the stories of this book have been changed and, in some cases, composite stories of real people have been used in order to protect individual privacy. In the cases of those who have given us permission to share them, real names have been used.

To order additional books:
www.amazon.com
www.aboutdads.org

Published by Anyman Publishing, LLC

ISBN: 978-1-952943-33-1

E-book also available

Editorial and Book Packaging: Inspira Literary Solutions, Gig Harbor, WA

Printed in the USA

*To the men of DADS—past, present, and future—
It has been one of the greatest honors of my life to walk alongside
you in the sacred work of fatherhood and reunification.
For the past 27 years, your resilience, hope, and love for your children
have been the living heartbeat of this mission.*

TABLE OF CONTENTS

Foreword   xiii
Introduction   1

Chapter 1	A New Frontier in Fatherhood	7
Chapter 2	Learning the Art of Listening	19
Chapter 3	A New Model for Fatherhood	29
Chapter 4	Mentoring and Being Mentored	41
Chapter 5	A Template for Fellowship	55
Chapter 6	Relationship Is Key	65
Chapter 7	Mitigating Risk Factors	73
Chapter 8	The Power of Community	83
Chapter 9	Steps on the Fatherhood Journey	95
Chapter 10	The Loss of My Father	105
Chapter 11	The Men of DADS	115
Chapter 12	God Will Provide	125
Chapter 13	Expanding the Vision of DADS	135

Acknowledgments   143
About the Author   145
Other Books by Marvin Charles   147

FOREWORD

There are few words more complex—and more needed in our conversation—than *father*. The word describes a role, a function, a necessary presence in the life of a child, and it carries expectations: progenitor, provider, protector, guide, teacher. However, these words describe what a father does, but the name *Father* is something different. It is relational; it speaks of engagement and commitment. It is not earned by function alone—it is conferred through presence, through love, through trust, and through belonging. A man may be called a father biologically, but to bear the name *Father* in a child's heart is to be a consistent presence and a grounding influence that makes the world a place of possibility and hope.

In the Scriptures, God chooses to be known not merely as Creator or King, but as Father—not simply the one who made us, but the one who longs for us, stays with us, and delights in calling us beloved. Moreover, it is the work of the Spirit, through the legacy of the prophet Elijah, that the hearts of human fathers are turned toward their children. This is our prayer today: that if we are to restore collective flourishing within our culture, the Spirit must help us heal the relationship between fathers and their children. In other words, the healing of the father-child relationship is connected to the healing—and the revolution—of the whole society. To reclaim the word *father* as a living name is at the heart of Marvin Charles's work—and it is one of the most urgent calls of our time.

My own experience with my father was shaped by a yearning to be seen and known by him—and for so many years of my life, he felt just out of reach. We lived in the same house and saw each other every day, but he had learned from his own father to be emotionally distant. While he was physically present, he was also relationally absent. Many of us have yearned to know our fathers' hearts, but have been wounded by their absence.

In a world marked by fracture, loneliness, and deep generational wounds, the absence of fathers has left a hollow place in our homes, our communities, and our collective spirit. The absence is not merely physical—it is emotional, spiritual, and communal. And yet, into that void, there are voices rising, calling us back to something sacred, something forgotten, something fiercely needed. Marvin Charles is one of those voices.

This book, *A DADS Revolution: Pass It On*, is not simply Marvin's story. It is a call to all of us—to remember who we are meant to be, to reckon with the stories that shaped us, and to dare to believe that healing is possible, even in places long abandoned. Marvin writes with the kind of authority that can only be born from suffering, from survival, and ultimately from surrender to a larger hope. He is not merely a survivor, but an overcomer—sharing with vulnerability his own story of struggle to become the father he wished he had. His story reminds us that redemption is not just an idea—it is an embodied movement. We must have skin in the game, and be humble enough to face our shame as we fail and try again. One person at a time, one relationship at a time—but never done alone. DADS is a testimony to this collective work.

What strikes me most about Marvin's work is that it is not driven by guilt or shame—it is fueled by hope. Hope that men can change. Hope that broken families can be mended. Hope that sons and daughters can grow up knowing they are seen, loved, and cherished. Hope that our communities, torn by abandonment and despair, can find new life through fathers who return—not perfectly, but faithfully.

Reading these pages, you will find practical wisdom, yes. You will hear stories of men who dared to have the courage to step back into the lives of their children. But more than anything, you will feel an invitation—an invitation to be part of a revolution. Not a revolution of force or domination, but a revolution of love, commitment, and presence. A revolution that begins quietly in the heart of a man who decides to stay, to listen, to heal. A revolution that not only heals the hearts of our children, but also our own—and even the hearts of our fathers, whom we begin to see in a different light.

I am grateful for Marvin and Jeanett Charles. I am grateful for the countless men who have walked through the doors of DADS and chosen a different path. And I am grateful for the chance to speak out about this revolution—one that our world desperately needs. For in this, we have hope: not just in our work, but in the redemptive and revolutionary work of the Spirit of God.

May you read this book not just with your mind, but with your heart. And may you find yourself drawn into the kind of story that can change generations. For this is how our hearts are softened, turned, and brought to hear the call of those who belong to us, and to whom we belong.

J. Derek McNeil, Ph.D.
President and Provost, The Seattle School of Theology & Psychology

INTRODUCTION

I grew up in the central district of Seattle as a teenager in the seventies, and although it was the "Summer of Love," the harsh reality was that love in any form was something unknown to me. In my youth, I lacked a positive father figure. Unbeknownst to me, my father was off serving in the Army, completely unaware of my existence.

After recurring brutal experiences as a ward of the state, I decided to play my hand at street life. The next few decades I spent on the streets, learning what it takes to make it as part of a drug syndicate. Among my friends on the street, my story was a common one. We all lacked a significant father figure in our lives. Ultimately, this created a void in us that drugs, alcohol, and the criminal justice system could not begin to fill.

A main cause of my reckless behavior was the absence of my father. Though I cannot necessarily attribute *all* of my struggles to fatherlessness, it's possible that without fatherlessness I'd be telling a completely different story today. I do tell my story, though, so someone else can be different.

Being a storyteller, my job isn't just to tell my own stories, but to listen to others as well. A massive part of my growth comes from listening to the stories of the fathers who come through DADS on their journeys to connect with their children. When working with these men, before we get to their children in the present, we help them examine their past upbringing with their own fathers. I've been privy to hundreds of support group sessions, and in every single one I've thought about how different someone's life may have turned out if they had known the worthiness of a father's love as opposed to his abandonment.

In reality, you cannot change the past, but you can take steps to change how you let it affect you.

As adolescents, so many young men are trying to determine who they are and whether they're able to stand on their own in the world. It's difficult to determine who you are without knowing where you came from. Biologically, a son is in many ways a physical replica of his father. The Y-chromosome sons receive from their father alone, along with height and other genetic material.

Growing up not knowing who my father was, I didn't know whom or where I came from. That pierced my identity, leaving a sense of loneliness where belonging could have been. The fact of the matter is that children—boys and girls both—need to have a sense of belonging associated with their identity. If not, they will go looking for a sense of belonging elsewhere, like I did.

Nevertheless, for some time there was no culture pertaining to fatherhood. It was never determined what were the responsibilities of a father, and how men were obligated to fulfill those duties. On the other hand, there is motherhood, a role with in-depth, articulated customs and ideals. When it comes to the topic of motherhood, there are various definitions and depictions of a mother's responsibilities.

What IS a dad, anyway?

INTRODUCTION

Sadly, most definitions and depictions of fatherhood these days are ambiguous to the point of being useless—sometimes even downright harmful. The lack of consistent messaging on fatherhood can lead to many men taking the path of least resistance and abandoning their role as a father altogether—especially men who didn't have a present father figure of their own to model after. This opens the door for misconceptions and stereotypes to creep in and take root in men's minds.

How can fathers be expected to succeed when they have been given no guidance, no direction, and no encouragement? And why is there a vacuum related to the overall awareness of the role of a father as opposed to a mother? We can focus on who or what may be responsible, or more importantly, we can focus on how we can eliminate that vacuum, with the end game of continuing to expand and improve the culture of fatherhood.

Today, if you walk down the street like I often do in Seattle, you will see the new millennial dads pushing their toddlers in strollers with their infants strapped to their chest. The fathers of today are present in their children's lives. They are in touch with their children not because they have to be but because they have a desire to be. The question is: what has prompted these men to take on fatherhood differently than their predecessors?

While there is an abundance of awareness on the topic compared to decades prior, fatherlessness is still infiltrating families across the world. Noticing the promise and new hope that the fathers of today can experience, there is a need to prioritize these men in their pursuit of fatherhood to prevent history from repeating itself, and to avoid the continuance of the cycle of trauma associated with absent fathers.

It's certainly evident that fathers don't have nearly as much parental support as mothers possess, due to lingering patriarchal standards on how men and women are "supposed" to care for their children. Past parenting ideologies have mostly depicted the father as the emotionally unavailable parent, the parent who supports the children within the household financially while all other aspects of parenthood remain ultimately the mother's responsibility. These past fatherhood paradigms are, in truth, completely underwhelming. Over time, this stigma has changed, thanks to the new fathers of today and new societal norms. These new norms establish new boundaries specific to manhood and an increasing role for men in parenting.

Another issue at hand has been that, over the years, there has been fundamental examination of what is sometimes referred to as "toxic" masculinity and its role in our society. Every young male has a presence of masculinity in his life, regardless of the amount. If that masculinity is toxic, it will set forth a negative presence within a man's life. Some examples of *actual* toxic masculinity are male stereotypes such as "boys don't cry," the belief that the ideal male is someone who does not actively show emotion in public. Toxic masculinity presents this caricature as being a "strong man" when, in reality, this is a man who is not emotionally mature and is bound to engage in irrational behavior.

I believe the younger generation of engaged fathers is creating an engaged fatherhood culture that differentiates between positive and toxic forms of masculinity. Positive masculinity allows men to present themselves in a way that channels vulnerability and confidence. The new fathers of today can express a wide range of emotions, be vulnerable, and seek guidance. This specifically helps a

INTRODUCTION

father identify his shortcomings and navigate the journey of manhood and fatherhood spiritually, to improve himself to break the cycle of trauma. This is the DADS revolution—and the paradigm we seek to emulate at DADS.

Clearly, the social atmosphere surrounding fatherhood has changed for the better, but still, fatherlessness exists. There is a duty to make sure there are resources for fathers to have an open dialogue about fatherhood, to make sure that the ideals of fatherhood are preserved. Men need to continue to reexamine their flaws because there is always room for improvement. There is a goal that fatherhood will be held in the same limelight as motherhood, that fatherhood will be regarded as in the same capacity as motherhood.

Don't get me wrong; I don't want people to consider fatherhood and motherhood as the same thing because they are not. However, I do want fathers to have the same resources as mothers. I particularly desire the idea of a father's love to be viewed as important as a mother's.

More than anything, I want the term "absentee father" to be eradicated.

With that in mind, I leave you with my second book, as the mission and ministry of D.A.D.S. (Divine Alternatives for Dads Services)—and my own fatherhood journey—continues.

Marvin Charles

CHAPTER 1

A New Frontier in Fatherhood

I was fifty-four years old when our daughter, Jamie Michelle, was born, and from that moment, my entire concept of fatherhood shifted in ways I never anticipated. Parenting her was a whole new frontier for my wife, Jeanett, and me. For one, our older children were now graduating from high school and heading off to college, and we found ourselves in this strange yet wonderful position of being empty nesters in one sense, yet full-time parents again in another.

The older seven children in our blended family grew up knowing struggle, tight budgets, and sacrifice as we navigated life in our younger years. But Jamie Michelle, our youngest, entered a much more stable family, both financially and emotionally, and with a completely different family dynamic. And perhaps most important of all, this was the first time I had the chance to fully parent a child from birth while married to her mother.

With my older kids, I was a single dad for much of their lives.[1] Jeanett and I were together during part of their upbringing, but we weren't married at the time. I didn't realize until much later just how significant that difference in my marital status would be in shaping my approach to fatherhood. With Jamie, from day one, I had the security of a committed marriage and a shared foundation of values, love, and stability. That changed the game for me in ways I'm still discovering. It's been a profound journey—both as a dad to Jamie and in how I've reconnected with my older kids, who, despite being grown, still need their father.

Parenting in Two Eras

I sometimes joke with Jeanett that it feels like I'm raising kids in two different eras, because in many ways, that's exactly what's happening. My older children, whom I fathered as a much younger man, experienced a vastly different world. When they were growing up, we were scraping by, piecing together a life that sometimes felt like a patchwork quilt. We lived on a budget so tight that luxuries were almost non-existent. Vacations were rare and modest; we drove used cars with over 100,000 miles on them and shopped at discount stores because that's what we could afford.

But it wasn't just our financial situation that made those years feel so different—it was also the fact that, back then, I was still figuring out how to be a dad. I was younger, less sure of myself, and to be honest, I deferred to Jeanett on almost everything. She

---

[1]. That story can be read in my first book, *Becoming DADS: A Mission to Restore Absent Fathers*, available on Amazon.com and anywhere books are sold.

was more confident, more consistent, and more experienced when it came to parenting. I often let her take the lead and leaned on her decisions because I didn't have the confidence to stand firm in my role.

I didn't realize it at the time, but that insecurity affected my relationship with the older kids. They knew I loved them, but they also knew I wasn't always the decision-maker or the one to run to with their emotional or practical needs. Jeanett filled that role more often than not.

Fast forward to seventy, and I'm a whole different man. I'm more confident, not only in my role as a father but in the marriage and family structure that surrounds me. Financially, we're more stable, which means we don't have to make the same sacrifices we did back in the day. Jamie's life is full of opportunities that I could only dream of offering my older kids when they were her age. I have more time and emotional bandwidth to be present with her in ways I wasn't able to for my other children. I can attend every game, every school function, and even have the luxury of spending time with her one-on-one, something that felt impossible years ago.

But it's not just the material things that make this second round of fatherhood different; it's the emotional presence. I'm not the same anxious young father who doubted himself at every turn. I'm not constantly questioning whether I'm doing it "right" or if I'm somehow failing her. And that change has made all the difference.

Reconnecting with My Older Kids

Parenting Jamie has given me new insights into what I may have missed with my older kids, but it has also been the key to reconnecting with them in deeper, more meaningful ways. In those early years, when I wasn't out of the picture due to my addictions, and when I was present in their lives, I was always focused on being a provider. That was my main focus. I worked as hard as I knew how to keep a roof over their heads, and food on their table, and to make sure they had what they needed—what we all needed—to survive. I was doing what I thought a father was supposed to do.

What I didn't realize then was how much they needed me emotionally, too. I didn't have the capacity to show up for them in the ways I wanted to, or rather, I didn't know how. I was always in motion, moving from one responsibility to the next. I rarely took the time to sit with them, ask how they were doing, or connect with them beyond the surface level.

Now, with Jamie, I've learned to slow down and prioritize our relationship. I'm intentional about spending time with her, whether it's helping with her homework, going shopping for school clothes, or just sitting down and talking. Those small acts of intentional care have had a big impact on her, and in turn, they've helped me realize what I missed with my older kids.

But here's the beautiful part—by being more present with Jamie, I've been able to re-engage with my older children in ways I never thought possible. I've had conversations with them that we never had when they were younger. I'm connecting with them emotionally, and they're seeing me in a new light—not just as "Dad, the provider," but as "Dad, the person."

One of the greatest lessons I've learned is that it's never too late to show up for your children. My sons and daughters are adults now, with their own lives and challenges, but that doesn't mean they've stopped needing their father. They need me in different ways, of course, but the need is still there. Being able to speak into their lives now—with the wisdom, patience, and confidence I didn't have when they were younger—has been a gift. I'm more comfortable communicating with them, offering advice, and supporting them in their personal and professional journeys.

I'm not afraid to have the tough conversations anymore, the ones where I ask them about their dreams, their goals, and what they need from me as their father. And more importantly, I'm able to listen in ways I couldn't before. I've found that my older kids have a lot to say now that they're adults, and being able to have those deep, meaningful conversations has brought us closer together.

Raising the Bar and the Tension of Change

One of the biggest challenges I've faced as a father of kids in two different generations is navigating the tension between where we were financially when my older children were growing up and where we are now. It's no secret that Jamie's life looks very different from theirs. While we were scraping by when the older kids were young, we're now in a much more comfortable position. Jamie has access to things that were once unimaginable for her siblings—private school, extracurricular activities, vacations, and other "perks."

This has sometimes created a sense of tension between the kids, particularly when the older ones perceive Jamie as being "spoiled." They've made comments about how she doesn't know what it's like to struggle, to go without. And they're not wrong.

But I've learned that it's important to acknowledge that difference without minimizing their experience. Yes, Jamie's life is easier in many ways, but that doesn't mean I love her any more than I loved them. It just means we're in a different place now.

What I've come to realize is that raising the bar for Jamie doesn't have to come at the expense of my older kids. In fact, it's made me more intentional about encouraging them to continue striving for their own goals. For one, I've had to update the conversations I have with them about what success looks like.

In our community, we sometimes set the bar too low. We say things like, "At least I didn't end up in prison," or, "At least I graduated high school." While those are important milestones, we can't stop there. I want my kids to know that they're capable of so much more—that their dreams and aspirations are valid, and that they don't have to settle for less just because they've overcome certain challenges.

It's about helping them dream bigger and believe that they're worthy of the opportunities that come their way. I didn't have the financial freedom to show them the world when they were younger, but I can invest in their dreams now. I can be there to support them emotionally, financially, and spiritually in ways that I couldn't before. And that's been a key part of reconnecting with them—trying to let them know that I'm still here for them, still rooting for them, still expecting great things from them.

I want them to know that their dreams are valid, their voices matter, and that they can count on me to be there, cheering them on every step of the way. That's the legacy I hope to leave as a father—one of love, expectation, and unwavering support.

Unpacking the Past and Moving Forward

Thankfully, there are people in my life whom I can talk to when I need help or feedback. I'm blessed to have those who will challenge me, encourage me, and help me grow. Fatherhood, especially later in life, is full of moments where I realize how much I still have to learn. Sometimes that means facing some hard truths about my past as a parent.

A few years ago, my daughter Marvette, our second youngest child, asked me to go to therapy with her. It took me by surprise, not because we'd never talked about hard things, but because it wasn't something I would have expected her to ask. I agreed, even though I wasn't entirely sure what to expect. I figured, whatever it was, I could handle it.

What I didn't realize was how much I would have to hear about myself—things I had never considered from her perspective. In that session, Marvette told me everything I had done wrong when she was growing up and how much it had impacted her. She told me how my decisions, my absence at times, and even my approach to discipline shaped her in ways I had never fully acknowledged.

I've got to be honest—it was uncomfortable. Listening to your child lay out her pain, especially when you know that pain has something to do with you, is a hard pill to swallow. As a father, I had always believed I was doing my best, doing what I thought was right. But sitting there with Marvette, hearing her describe the consequences of my actions, I realized that my best hadn't always been enough for her.

The therapist told me something that stuck with me: I needed to let her feel the way she feels. She said that part of Marvette's healing process was about me accepting her truth, even if it was hard for me to hear. And that hit me. I had spent so much time believing I had to be strong for my kids, be the authority, the provider. I didn't realize that part of being a good father was also learning how to listen and how to hold space for their feelings, even when those feelings were about me.

It was humbling. I told Marvette right there that I was willing to go with her to therapy every week until she felt we had resolved it—until she felt the healing she needed. I made that offer because I wanted her to know I was committed, that I was all in. She didn't ask me to do that, and she didn't take me up on it, but that conversation opened my eyes to something I hadn't fully grasped before: the weight of my fatherhood, and how much of an impact I'd had on my children, both good and bad.

Making Amends and Moving Forward

Not long after that, my son, Marvin Jr., came to see me. He and his sister, Marvette, showed up at my office together, both of them carrying something heavy that needed to be put down. They told me they needed to reconcile some things with me from our past. I could tell they had been thinking about this for a while, and I was ready to hear them out.

We sat down, and Marvin Jr. started talking. He said, "Dad, I'm just trying to get my grind on. I'm really upset about some stuff, and I remember you telling me to suck it up when I was younger. So that's what I've been doing."

That hit me like a ton of bricks. I remembered those words. I said them so casually back then, not thinking much about it. "Suck it up." It was something I had been told by my own father and others, and it was the only way I knew how to respond to adversity. You tough it out, push through, and move on. But hearing Marvin repeat those words to me made me realize how wrong I had been.

I told him that day, "Son, I was wrong to say that. I've learned better since then. Sucking it up is not the way to handle things. We need to talk about the stuff we're going through, be vulnerable with the people who care about us." I wanted him to know that the way I parented him in the past was based on what I knew then, but I've grown since those days. I'm not the same man, and I've learned that bottling things up only causes more pain in the long run.

Marvin Jr. and I had a real conversation that day, one where I apologized for the times I had failed him as a father. It wasn't an easy talk, but it was necessary. I realized that my kids—now adults—still carry the weight of the things I said and did when they were younger. And it wasn't just Marvin. Marvette had her own hurts, too. Both of them needed to hear that I was willing to own my mistakes and that I was open to healing those wounds.

That conversation marked a turning point in our relationship. I told both Marvin Jr. and Marvette that I was here to listen, to be the father they needed now, not just the one I was back then. I've been working on things with them and their other siblings ever since, slowly but surely mending the gaps that time, miscommunication, and generational expectations had created.

Breaking the Cycle

One of the most challenging things I've come to realize is how much generational patterns play a role in fatherhood. When I look at Marvin Jr. and my other kids, I can see some of the same struggles they face as parents that I experienced when I was their age. Some of it stems from the way I raised them, but a lot of it goes deeper—back to what I experienced growing up, and what my parents and grandparents experienced before me.

For example, Marvin Jr. reminds me so much of myself at his age. He's driven, hardworking, and focused, but he's also holding on to a lot of unresolved emotions. I see the same patterns I went through—pushing through, not talking about things, keeping it all inside because that's what we were taught to do. It's a cycle that has passed down from generation to generation in our family and in our community.

I can't tell you how many times we used the word "drama" when I was growing up. Whenever something went wrong, whenever there was a conflict, we'd call it drama. That was the term we used to describe everything—from family fights to financial stress. It was just a part of life. But now, with more understanding and awareness, I see that a lot of what we called "drama" was actually *trauma*.

The things we went through weren't just inconveniences or misunderstandings—they were traumatic experiences that left deep scars. And because we didn't know how to talk about it, we just stuffed it down, called it drama, and moved on. That's how I raised my boys, too. I taught them to be tough, to keep their emotions in check, to "man up" and handle things. But what I've learned—what I know now—is that manning up doesn't mean burying your feelings. It means facing them head-on, talking about them, and finding ways to heal.

I've had conversations with my kids about this new understanding of trauma. I've told them that I got it wrong back then.

What I thought was strength was actually avoidance. And I don't want them to carry that same burden. I want them to break the cycle, to be able to talk about their struggles, to seek help when they need it, and to recognize that being vulnerable doesn't make you weak—it makes you human.

A New Paradigm at DADS

This shift in perspective hasn't just changed the way I father my own children—it's also transformed the way we work with the men who come to us at DADS (Divine Alternatives for Dads Services). In our community, there's been a long-standing belief that men have to be stoic, that we have to bear our burdens in silence and never show weakness. That belief has done so much damage to generations of men, especially Black men. It's left us with emotional wounds that we never learned how to heal.

At DADS, we're teaching men a new way. We're helping them understand that trauma is real and that it needs to be addressed, not buried. We're showing them that they can be strong and vulnerable at the same time. We're modeling what it means to talk about your struggles and seek help, whether that's through therapy, mentorship, or simply opening up to a trusted friend.

This new outlook has been crucial, not just for the men who come through our doors but for me as well. I'm learning alongside them. I'm sharing my own journey of growth with them—how I've come to realize that the "tough it out" mentality I was raised with isn't serving us anymore. We need a new way of thinking, one that allows us to deal with the trauma we've experienced so we can be better fathers, husbands, and men.

Moving Forward

As I continue to father my children, and now have also taken on the role of grandfather (a new joy!), I'm learning to give myself grace. I made mistakes. I wasn't always the father I wanted to be, but I'm committed to doing better now. I'm committed to listening, to being vulnerable, and to healing the wounds of the past.

It's a journey, one that I'm still on, but I'm grateful for the opportunity to grow and to show my children that it's never too late to change, and to walk this journey with them and the community at DADS. We can break the cycles of trauma and, with God's help, build something new—something stronger and more loving—for the next generation. And that's the legacy I hope to leave as a father and as a leader in my community.

PASS IT ON

When we recognize that God's nature is inherently good, this understanding shapes our trust in Him and His plans for our lives.

> *Before I was afflicted I went astray,*
> *but now I obey your word.*
> *You are good, and what you do is*
> *good; teach me your decrees.*
> (Psalm 119:67-68)

CHAPTER 2

Learning the Art of Listening

What I'd like to share with you now is how we at DADS got to where we are currently—our motivations, the choices we made, and the journey we took. Things have changed significantly from how they looked when Jeanett and I first started out in ministry from our own kitchen table, and even since my first book, *Becoming DADS: A Mission to Restore Absent Fathers*, was published in 2016.

As the vision grew, our top priority question was, "How do we get the community involved?" To get buy-in from the community, we had to test our approach. We needed to gather the men we were serving, who were facing similar situations and who were willing to do whatever it took to make a difference in their own lives, so that they might make a difference in the lives of their children.

So, we started simple, and we put men with similar struggles together in the same room. At first, everyone looked around, wondering, *Why are we here? What are we doing?* This model was unheard of within the community,[2] especially at the early stages of our organization. But one thing became clear—each man shared a deep desire to be a father to his children. But no one was listening to them.

This realization was a pivotal moment because we were able to demonstrate to these men that even though nobody else was listening, they could listen to each other. Before that day, nobody would have admitted it, but none of those men wanted to be on this journey alone.

Twenty years earlier, when we started, we had no idea that simply listening to each other would be where the real change would begin. Today, I still hear men say, "I thought I was all alone." That's the stumbling block. They're not alone. You're not alone. In fact, most men who share this experience also start by thinking they're on their own.

Drama as Trauma

At DADS, much of our work involves helping men process trauma. When men walk through our doors, we don't tell them to just be strong and push through. Instead, we meet them where they are and ask, "What are you going through? How can we support you?"

---

2. For those unfamiliar with this usage of the word, "the community" is a term commonly used within the African American population to refer to the collective Black experience, culture, and shared social space in the city. This phrase encapsulates a sense of belonging, historical continuity, and cultural identity, often centered around historically Black neighborhoods, businesses, churches, and community organizations.

For many of these men, it's the first time in their lives that someone has asked those questions.

I remember the first time Derrick joined us in the group. He sat in the circle, his arms crossed, his body stiff. A room full of men talking about their feelings? That was definitely not his thing! He had spent years behind bars, learning that silence was safer. Words could be twisted, used against you. Vulnerability was a weakness.

But here he was, at a DADS meeting, because his parole officer thought it was a good idea. Because he had a son he barely knew. Because something deep inside him whispered that maybe, just maybe, he didn't want to be the kind of father his own had been—absent, angry, unreachable.

One of our mentors, Steve, was sitting across him, an older white man. He was quiet too, but for different reasons. Steve is the kind of guy who carries himself with a quiet strength, but there's a lot of lived experience and wisdom beneath his calm exterior. He had been where Derrick was, emotionally—for different reasons, but he recognized the signs.

The first few meetings, Derrick barely said a word. Steve noticed but never pushed. He just listened every time Derrick did speak.

One evening, after a particularly heavy discussion about childhood trauma, Derrick walked out of the meeting. Steve found him outside on the sidewalk, pacing, his fists clenched. Steve joined him but said nothing at first.

Then, Steve spoke. "I used to hate my father."

Derrick looked at him, startled. Steve continued, his voice steady. "Hated him for leaving, for drinking, for making my mom cry. And when I got older, I promised I'd never be like him. But then . . . I made my own mistakes."

Derrick didn't know if he was ready to let it all out. Could Steve be trusted? Knowing that Steve had shared experiences—even though they might not look exactly the same—helped Derrick lower his walls just a bit. For the first time, he later told me, he wondered what it would feel like to be truly heard. Not judged. Not lectured. Just heard. Steve invited him back into the meeting. And that night, for the first time, Derrick spoke in the group about his personal experiences. His words came slowly, haltingly, but they came. Steve—and all the men—listened, nodding, letting him know that his story mattered. That he mattered.

In the weeks that followed, Derrick learned that listening wasn't just about hearing words—it was about making space for someone else's pain, just as Steve had made space for his. It was about showing up, being present, being transparent. Derrick later shared that he wanted to let his son know—one day, when he was ready—that he would always be there, ears open, heart open, for him too.

At DADS, we are not just about teaching men to be fathers. We are about making room for all backgrounds, all walks of life, and, most importantly: healing—and healing starts with learning the art of listening. The reason listening is so powerful is that it allows men to begin that necessary process of healing. When a man feels heard, he can start to unpack his trauma. He can start to make sense of the things that have happened to him, rather than just stuffing them down and pretending they don't matter.

The problem with calling those life experiences "drama" is that it minimizes the impact of what's happening. It makes it seem like it's just a temporary inconvenience or a nuisance, rather than something that needs to be dealt with on a deeper level, something that needs to be listened to and "heard," before anything else.

Changing the Conversation

Understanding the difference between trauma and drama is crucial for the men we work with. When you label something as drama, the expectation is that you just get over it, move on, and stop complaining. But when you recognize something as trauma, you acknowledge that it needs to be addressed, worked through, and healed. Trauma isn't something you can just push aside. It sticks with you, festering, until you deal with it.

At DADS, we've started to change that conversation. We talk about trauma because that's what many of these men are dealing with. Childhood abuse, neglect, violence, poverty—these aren't just "dramatic" moments. They are traumatic experiences that shape how a person sees the world and themselves.

We've seen it time and time again at DADS. A man walks in, full of anger and frustration, convinced that no one cares about him or his story. But when we listen—really listen—he starts to soften. He starts to trust. And that's when the real work begins. Once a man feels heard, he's more willing to take the next step: addressing his trauma, learning new ways to cope, and ultimately becoming a better father for his own children.

This is especially important for absentee fathers. Many of the men we work with at DADS have been disconnected from their children for years. They feel ashamed, unworthy, and unsure of how to reconnect. But when they realize that their own trauma is part of what's holding them back, they can start to change. They can start to heal, and in doing so, they can become the fathers their children need.

As we continue this work at DADS, we are constantly reminded of how deeply trauma affects men's ability to be present for their children. Trauma doesn't just disappear when you become a father—it often intensifies. Many of the men we work with are haunted by their pasts, and those unhealed wounds make it difficult for them to be the fathers they want to be.

But the good news is that healing is possible. By creating a space where men can share their stories, confront their pain, and be heard, we're helping them break free from the cycles of trauma that have held them back for so long. It's not easy work, and it doesn't happen overnight, but it's worth it. Every time a father comes to us and tells us that he's starting to reconnect with his children, that he's learning to be present for them, we know we're on the right track.

What we've learned through all of this is that trauma isn't something that can be dealt with in isolation. It needs to be brought into the light, spoken about, and processed in community. That's what we're doing at DADS—building a community where men can face their trauma, heal, and become the fathers their children deserve.

When Men Feel Heard

When men come to us, they usually have a long list of reasons why they can't be good fathers or why they feel like they've failed as men. But when you peel back those layers, what you find is a deep sense of isolation and pain. Most guys coming through our doors say, "Nobody is listening to me!"

Johnnie, one of the leaders of our DADS community and a longtime friend of mine, often says, "What do we do at DADS? We listen." It's simple, but powerful.

Johnnie's own story reflects this. He grew up feeling like no one ever heard him. His father was a dark presence in his early life, and his mother was overwhelmed and distant because of her own trauma. As a teenager, Johnnie was frequently in trouble, acting out in ways that seemed inexplicable to those around him. But no one ever asked him why. They just told him to behave, to "straighten up and fly right," as if that were an easy fix.

Years later, after becoming involved with DADS, Johnnie realized the power of being heard. He once told me, "When someone finally heard me, when they really listened to what I was going through, it was like a weight being lifted off my shoulders." That's the foundation of what we do now at DADS. We listen, because we know how important it is for these men to feel like their voices matter.

I think back to my own experience. When I was fourteen, I cut my school principal. It's not a moment I'm proud of, but it's a pivotal part of my story. What people didn't know at the time was that I was dealing with a lot of unresolved trauma. My home life was unstable, and I was carrying more anger and pain than a teenager should have to handle. But nobody asked what was going on inside my head. They just saw a violent, troubled kid.

When I was expelled, there was no conversation about what led up to that moment. There was no one to help me process what I was feeling or why I had acted out. No one was there to listen.

I was simply labeled a problem, another statistic in a system that didn't care about the root causes of my pain.

Fast forward to my senior year, after I had been transferred to an alternative high school. There, the vice principal, Mrs. Valerie Colasurdo (who was white, incidentally), demonstrated extraordinary kindness to me. She brought me into her own home and allowed me to live there for a while with her and her husband and children during a particularly vulnerable time in my life. I later asked her how I could possibly repay her. She simply said, "Pass it on." That short phrase stuck in my mind, becoming a motto for my life and the subtitle for this book.

It wasn't until years later, when I was well into adulthood, that I started to unpack the anger and inner turmoil I carried as a kid. I realized that my inability to express myself, to have someone listen to me, had been a significant factor in the way my life played out. If just one person had taken the time to ask me what was going on back then, maybe things would have been different. Maybe I wouldn't have had to carry so much weight on my shoulders for so long. That revelation fuels much of the work I do at DADS.

Blake's Story

At DADS, I've seen so many men with stories like Derrick's, Steve's, mine, and Johnnie's. One that stands out is Blake, a young man who came to us after being accused of some terrible things. Blake was devastated, not only by the accusation itself, but by the fact that no one was willing to listen to his side of the story. He was isolated, alone, and angry. When he first came to us, he didn't trust anyone. Why would he? In his mind, the world had already judged him.

We didn't rush to offer solutions or tell him what he needed to do to fix his life. Instead, we asked him to share his story. At first, he was hesitant. But over time, as he realized we weren't there to judge him, he started to open up. He talked about his childhood, how he had been neglected and abused. He shared how he had always felt like an outsider in his own family, never truly accepted or loved.

It became clear that the accusation, while serious, was part of a larger narrative of trauma and misunderstanding. Whether or not Blake was guilty wasn't our role to decide. What we were there to do was listen, to help him process the layers of pain and confusion that had led him to this point. And that's exactly what we did. We listened, and slowly, Blake began to heal. He realized that his story mattered, and for the first time in his life, he felt heard.

This is the kind of work we do at DADS now. We listen to lower the barriers men have built up over the years—the emotional walls they've put up to protect themselves from a world that has often failed them. Whether it's absentee fathers, men who have been in and out of the prison system, or those who've simply lost their way, the one common thread we've found is that these men feel like no one is listening to them.

When society tells you to just suck it up and get on with it, you start to believe that your feelings don't matter. You start to internalize the idea that being a man means bearing your pain in silence. But we know now that this approach doesn't work. It leads to broken families, broken communities, and men who are unable to be the fathers their children need.

At DADS, we've learned that the first step to helping men become better fathers is helping them find their voices. We encourage them to talk about their experiences, their trauma, their pain. We create a space where they can be vulnerable without fear of judgment. And in doing so, we begin to dismantle the old coping mechanisms that have kept them trapped in cycles of anger, frustration, and shame.

> **PASS IT ON**
>
> Listening is a foundational skill for effective communication and relationship building. It requires humility and a willingness to understand others before expressing our own views.
>
> *My dear brothers and sisters, take note of this:*
> *Everyone should be quick to listen, slow to*
> *speak and slow to become angry.*
> *(James 1:19)*

CHAPTER 3

A New Model for Fatherhood

The old model of fatherhood in our community was one of stoicism. Men were expected to be strong, to provide, and to keep their emotions in check. But that model has failed us in many ways. It's led to generations of men who are disconnected from their feelings, from their families, and from themselves. At DADS these days, we're building a new model, one that encourages men to be vulnerable, to talk about their trauma, and to seek healing. We believe that by helping men process their pain, we can help them become better fathers, husbands, and community members. This isn't about making men weak—it's about making them whole. It's about giving them the tools they need to break the cycles of trauma that have been passed down through generations. And it all starts with listening.

As we continue to evolve at DADS, we're finding that this new model for fatherhood doesn't just help the men who walk through our doors. It's transforming our entire community. As we work with fathers who are learning to face their pasts, we see them becoming more engaged not only in their children's lives but in the lives of those around them. The skills we're teaching—being vulnerable, facing trauma, expressing emotions—are rippling outward into families and neighborhoods, creating healthier relationships and stronger connections.

But it all starts with that first step: listening.

We've seen firsthand how the cycle of silence and unprocessed trauma passes from generation to generation. It's something that has impacted not only the men we serve but also our own lives. I've reflected a lot on this in my own journey, especially now that I'm parenting later in life.

At DADS, we now emphasize the importance of teaching men to listen, both to themselves and to others. Many of the men who come to us have never had anyone listen to them, but they've also never been taught how to listen to their own children, partners, or even their own inner voice. They've learned to bury their feelings, to numb their pain, and to stay silent.

One of our biggest challenges is helping these men break free from that silence. It's not an easy process. Many of them have been taught their whole lives that showing emotion is a sign of weakness. They've been told to hide their pain, to soldier on, and to keep their struggles to themselves. But we're trying to show them that strength doesn't come from silence—it comes from vulnerability. It comes from being able to say, "I'm hurting," and from being able to hear those words from someone else.

We've developed workshops and group sessions where the focus is on listening. We encourage the men to share their stories, but we also teach them how to listen to others. This has been a game-changer for many of them. They start to realize that they're not alone in their struggles, that other men are going through similar experiences. And by listening to each other, they begin to build a sense of community, trust, and support.

The Ripple Effect: Better Fathers, Better Communities

One of the most rewarding aspects of this work has been seeing the impact it has on these men's relationships with their children. When fathers learn to listen to their own pain and process their trauma, they become more equipped to listen to their kids. This has been particularly true for absentee fathers who have struggled to reconnect with their children after years of distance.

We've seen fathers who, for years, didn't know how to approach their kids or how to rebuild those broken relationships. But after spending time at DADS, after learning the art of listening and vulnerability, they've been able to go back to their children and say, "I'm sorry. I wasn't there for you, but I'm here now, and I want to listen to what you need." Those words have the power to heal wounds that may have seemed impossible to repair.

One father who stands out in my mind is Thomas. He had been in and out of prison for most of his adult life and had little contact with his children during that time. When he first came to DADS, he was full of regret. He felt like he had lost any chance of being a father to his kids. But over time, through our program, he began to understand the power of listening.

He worked on his own trauma, facing the abuse and neglect he had experienced as a child. As he did this, he became more comfortable opening up to his own kids. He started writing letters to them, sharing his story and letting them know that he wanted to be a part of their lives. And when he finally had the chance to meet with them in person, he didn't come in with answers or expectations. He just listened.

Thomas told me later that his meeting with his children was one of the most powerful moments of his life. For the first time, he wasn't trying to control the conversation or fix things. He was just present, hearing what his kids had to say. And in that space of listening, they were able to start rebuilding their relationship. It's still a work in progress, but the foundation has been laid.

What I Wish I Knew Then, I'm Learning Now

I was talking to a friend recently about things we never learned in school, like how to pay bills or handle life skills. No one teaches us the art of listening either; it's something I learned through trial and error. I didn't grow up with it, and I didn't even understand the value of it until years later. At first, I just wanted to prove my point, like so many other men do. But trying to prove my point kept me from actually being heard.

I wish someone had explained this to me sooner. I remember leaving a courtroom angry one day, asking, "Why can't I have my kids?" I wasn't thinking about my past actions, the things that had put me in this position. Instead, I just wanted people to believe I was capable of being a father. But the courts saw things differently. They were responsible for protecting my children, and they needed proof that I could be trusted. This was a hard pill to swallow, but it became clear that I needed to reestablish myself, to show the courts who I could become.

After a court hearing one day, when I was trying to put my family back together, a woman from the court followed me outside one day and said to me, "Can I give you some advice? You're paying attention to everyone in that courtroom. The only person you really need to focus on is the judge." That advice changed my life. I realized I needed to prove myself to the judge, not worry about everyone else. So, I started doing everything necessary—taking classes, re-creating myself, and showing up in new ways.

It was one of the best pieces of advice I ever received.

Today, I tell men that being in DADS' programs, and taking parenting classes, is all part of reestablishing themselves. They're learning new skills that they didn't have before, and over time, that effort starts to hold weight. They are creating a new reputation, and with that comes the chance to show their kids the father they want to be.

The Impact of Our Innovative Fatherhood Curriculum

After I wrote and published *Becoming DADS: A Mission to Restore Absent Fathers*, an opportunity arose for me to develop our *Becoming Dads Innovative Fatherhood Curriculum*, with the help of family life education expert Dr. George Williams, PhD. This curriculum exponentially expanded our reach, and our ability to systematically teach men both the practical skills and the soft skills they need to grow into connected, invested fathers.

This curriculum helps participants build the knowledge base, adjust attitudes, and apply skills related to becoming the dads their children need, including:

- Facing the truth of their past and having hope for a better future
- Understanding the impact of their role as a father
- Knowing what their children need from them
- Being committed to their children for a lifetime
- Understanding the character of a man who lives for others
- Knowing how to have a healthy relationship with their child's mother
- Starting on the road to healing and getting past hurdles to effective fathering
- Being grounded in their spiritual walk with God
- Improving their employment situation
- Navigating the child support system
- Getting on track to providing child support

During the course, the men learn and recite "The DADS Pledge," which is as follows:

BECOMING A BETTER DAD

*To become a better dad,
I will turn my life around,
face the truth, and break free from the things
that at one time held me down.*

*To become a better dad,
I will commit to being there
for the sake of my child
by investing this time here.*

*To become a better dad,
I will do what men do:
mature, respect women, love and serve others.
And that includes my children too.*

*To become a better dad,
I need healing from my past—
all the hurt, trauma, and failures—
forgiving, making amends, moving forward at last.*

*To become a better dad,
I will be humble and seek to learn
ways to improve as a parent, co-parent, and citizen,
and let this passion to be better burn.*

*I will become a better dad,
no matter how tough; I won't quit or give up,
through the support of my faith, family, and community,
until my last breath and my eyes finally shut.*

Helping their child develop in every way requires the commitment of being there. Fathering is rewarding but also requires hard work. And without commitment, hard work does not get done. In these classes, men learn tangible skills and life principles that equip them for the hard work of fatherhood. Over the course of the classes, the men learn what commitment really is—and what it can and should look like. It is an action word. It something to embrace, not to avoid. This is a new paradigm for many of our men.

New Beginnings

The men who graduate from these classes share powerful declarations of their resolve to be the father who is there for his children. One of my favorite things is seeing them walk across the stage at graduation time. Another, even more poignant, is when several of them address our supporters at our annual DADS banquet held each June in Seattle, around Father's Day.

This past June, guests clapped as the honorees took the stage one by one, some with their children in their arms or standing next to them at the podium. Their stories were inspiring to all—like Ernest, who said, "I came out of a life of incarceration and addiction into a life of freedom." His young daughter was with him, smiling happily.

Suleiman held his two-year-old son in his arms and spoke of "being held accountable" as a father, and how that had changed his mindset. Bailey had participated in the DADS course via Zoom, but drove up from Portland for this event. He told the audience, which was clearly moved, "I grew up without a father. And I've learned how being there for your kids in good times and tough times is what being a father is all about."

Abraham shared how he had found his young son in a precarious position in a gang house, with the child's drug-addicted mother. We helped Abraham quickly secure an emergency parenting plan and rescue his son. "I'm so grateful for everything that DADS has done," he said.

Generally, working with these fathers, I find that I must listen more deeply than most people would in a typical agency. Usually, in other organizations, an intake form is filled out, information is gathered, and the case is sent down the chain. But that's not how we do it at DADS. From the moment someone walks in our door, we're committed to understanding where each person, individually, truly is and where he wants to go.

For example, a man might come in saying, "I want to see my kids; I want to be involved in their lives." So, I'll ask him to tell me more. Usually, what I hear next is a long list of reasons why he can't see his kids—mostly focused on the mother of his children. He might talk for thirty minutes, saying, "She won't let me," or "She's always in the way." But he never actually mentions the kids.

After those thirty minutes, I'll gently remind him, "You said you wanted to see your kids because you love them. But in all this time, you haven't mentioned them once." If I were a judge, it would be hard to believe that his kids mean the world to him if he's not even talking about them. This is where the art of listening comes in, and I try to teach him that skill.

I had to learn how to navigate these conversations myself, back when I was in their shoes. I had to be okay with not being heard in the way I wanted but instead, focus on being heard in the way that would benefit me most—and that is how we direct the men at DADS to focus as well.

Catching Men's Stories

This is why we developed our StoryCatcher® program at DADS; it is a simple but powerful tool that is helping to transform lives. This innovative app is more than just a piece of technology; it's a bridge of communication, a mirror for self-reflection, and a means of preserving the often-unheard stories of fatherhood. Through the StoryCatcher, we record each man's story, asking meaningful questions and letting them answer honestly. This teaches them to listen to themselves and reflect on their responses.

Many of the men who come through DADS carry untold stories—of struggle, of resilience, of lessons learned the hard way. The program uses StoryCatcher to invite these fathers to share their thoughts and experiences. With a few taps on a screen, men can record personal video stories, reflect on their own fathers or father figures, and begin to articulate the kind of dad they want to become. The process is therapeutic and empowering. It gives men a voice, and more importantly, it gives them ownership over their narrative.

Perhaps the most meaningful aspect of using StoryCatcher within DADS is the opportunity it creates for connection. Fathers can choose to share their stories with their children, family members, or peers. In doing so, they're not only capturing memories but also modeling vulnerability, self-awareness, and love—key ingredients of intentional fatherhood.

This skill of listening, starting with listening to themselves, is crucial because it has long-term benefits. When these men truly learn to listen, their kids eventually learn to listen to them, too. Their significant others start listening, and they themselves begin to navigate conversations differently. It's about breaking through. And I tell these men that I went through this same process. I didn't skip any steps, and neither will they. This journey will help their kids someday.

For many men, the biggest hurdle is building an image of fatherhood, often without any role model of their own to follow. This is what I remind them: maybe no one ever gave you this opportunity, but now you have the chance to create that father figure within yourself. A father's job, I always say, is to prepare his children for a future he'll never see. That's what this journey is about.

Looking back over twenty-five plus years, I can see how far we've come. People call me all the time to say, "Hey OG, it's still working." They tell me that they're still using what I taught them, and some have even started fatherhood programs of their own. One young man I worked with obtained custody of his first child, and then ten years later, of his second. He now runs a fatherhood program where he throws baby showers for fathers. He told me, "Why do we wait until after the baby arrives to acknowledge the father? Let's start before the baby gets here." It's powerful to see men investing in fatherhood earlier, knowing they have a support system.

This work is all about creating opportunities for these men to step into their roles as fathers and learn what it truly means to be there for their children. And it wouldn't be possible without listening to these men and helping them learn how to do the same for one another—and for their children.

PASS IT ON

The turning of hearts signifies the importance of passing down faith and values from one generation to the next.

He will turn the hearts of the parents to their children,
and the hearts of the children to their parents…
(Malachi 4:6)

CHAPTER 4

Mentoring and Being Mentored

One important way we've incorporated the practice of listening, in the context of building supportive relationships, is through active mentoring. Mentoring, at its core, is about guidance, support, and wisdom passed from one person to another. It's about one person sharing their experiences, successes, and mistakes to help someone else avoid the pitfalls that life inevitably throws our way.

In my seventy years, I've learned that mentoring isn't just about giving advice—it's about being a steady presence, a listening ear, and sometimes, simply showing what it looks like to walk the path of life with integrity and purpose. For many men in the community in which I grew up, and really, in society at large, this kind of guidance has not always been readily available, especially when it comes to learning how to be a husband and father.

I know firsthand how powerful mentoring can be. When I was a young man, I didn't have the best examples of fatherhood or marriage in my life. Very few of the significant males in my life were emotionally present—they didn't talk about feelings. They didn't teach me how to express love or how to build a healthy relationship. Like many men in our community, I had to figure out a lot of that on my own. But I have been blessed along the way to have older men in my life who took an interest in me, who showed me what it meant to be a man of character, to love and respect my wife, and to raise my children with care and intentionality.

Life-on-Life Impact

In many ways, I've come to view fatherhood and mentorship as interconnected concepts with various facets. A young boy grows up through stages: from boyhood to childhood, then to teenhood, adulthood, and eventually manhood. These dynamics are significant. For this growth to happen in a healthy way, healthy guidance is essential. Of course, one would hope that most of this occurs in a supportive family environment and with a strong father-child bond. Sadly, that is often not the case. That's where mentorship can come in and serve that purpose.

However, mentorship was a concept I didn't understand at all until it was introduced to me as an adult. I had no clue where it started or how it developed. In fact, it wasn't until I became a man and experienced it firsthand that I began to grasp what mentorship truly was.

The initial stages of mentorship involve understanding and empathy—someone has to show you what it means to care before you can comprehend the value of mentorship in your life. People mentor those they care about, or those whom they feel could benefit from their guidance. If you haven't experienced genuine care, you might not recognize it when it's offered.

For me, people in my old life often used phrases like, "I care for you," or, "I love you," in a superficial way. The way they expressed care came with no real expectations of how they would actually relate to me or I to them. I internalized this superficiality and carried it over to how I treated others, without realizing it could impact greatness or success. I was unaware of how profound this dynamic of caring, life-on-life, could be.

When I was a young man, there was a man I admired named Michael Waters. I looked up to him as if he were a god—not because of his actual achievements, but because of his eloquence and ability to persuade others. In my early twenties, how well you spoke and convinced others was a significant aspect of the lifestyle I was involved in.

Despite my respect for him, Michael seemed to go out of his way to belittle my achievements—at least, that was what it felt like to me. At the time, I felt like he was always talking down to me and rubbing his "success" in my face. I'd later learn that this was something he saw as a test of character and was part of his way of trying to mentor me, as misguided as that was. He ended up serving time in San Quentin and changing his name. I saw him again after he got out and he told me he was proud of me. Honestly, this was the first time anyone affirmed me in a way that felt earned and deserved. Although, sadly, Michael was murdered years ago, I often think about him and the lessons he imparted to me. Obviously, he was not a role model in any practical way that now we might consider appropriate, because of his lifestyle. That being said, my relationship with Michael Waters planted the seed in me of the value of life-on-life impact.

Today, I apply these lessons differently. I too test people's abilities, not in the same harsh way Michael did, but to prepare them for challenges. One mentor once told me to love all people, even those who were difficult. When I asked how to do this, he advised me to "lean in" instead of seeing their issues merely as problems. By understanding their struggles and empathizing, you can help them navigate their challenges. By getting closer to them and their situation, instead of pulling back, they will feel supported instead of judged and it can make their victories feel like your victories. Some of the techniques for handling other people's problems I learned on the streets still apply today, though they are now framed as mentoring and fathering. My experiences have allowed me to refine these approaches and use them to build others up effectively.

For instance, when I first worked with my valued colleague at DADS, Larry Brooks, I tested his abilities to ensure he could handle tough situations. If something ever happens to me, I need to know Larry can wisely and skillfully deal with it. Clients often come to us with serious issues, and they need to be mentored and guided through their difficulties. Larry has stood the test and demonstrated he has what it takes. Many of those skills he learned in the mentoring relationship I've had with him over the years and I am so grateful for the impact he's had on me as well.

My goal in mentoring is to help men develop the resilience they need to handle challenges with their own children. To me, that's the greatest honor—seeing someone grow in a way that equips them to handle their responsibilities effectively. Looking back, I didn't foresee any of this. Twenty-six years ago, I had no idea what the future held. All I had was determination and a strong desire to keep moving forward, despite having no money or resources. That determination, guided by God's direction and provision, has led us to where we are today.

The question now is whether I can pass on the same determination to others, mentoring them and helping them advance. A crucial part of this process is ensuring that once someone succeeds, they also help others in the same way. It's about continuing the cycle of mentorship and support.

I'll Walk with You

One of the main aspects of mentoring is being able to walk alongside others through uncertainty. This principle not only applies with our clients at DADS, but also applies to our student groups and staff meetings. Authenticity is key in mentorship, and while it's a buzzword these days, genuinely embodying it is crucial. It's about inviting others to be vulnerable through your own vulnerability. This approach goes beyond just providing guidance; it involves truly listening and meeting people where they are. Often, people are "talked at" rather than with, especially in support settings. The reality is, we have tools, but they're meaningless if we don't personally acknowledge that we don't have all the answers.

One of our team members, James, a student of clinical psychology, sat down to talk with me about how the principles of authentic listening and mentorship have impacted his work. He told me:

> *"Marvin, my work with men has become more effective because I have learned to listen deeply and walk through uncertainty with my clients, rather than offering immediate*

solutions—and I learned this approach from observing you during our Bible studies. When someone was vulnerable, you'd say directly, 'I don't know, but I'll walk with you.'

This approach was both powerful and humble. You would offer support through hugs and prayer, sharing silence and acknowledging the struggles without pretending to have all the answers. This humility and willingness to be vulnerable yourself helped break down barriers and made the healing process more genuine. I realized that being open about my own struggles and not having all the answers allowed me to connect more deeply with others. This approach has been transformative, not only for me but for those I work with."

James' testimony humbled me; it is a powerful affirmation of the work we are doing with men at DADS. We are acknowledging that healing is a shared process, and that both parties benefit from this mutual support. We're all in this together.

For many, especially men who have been chronically ignored, finding someone who will walk with them through their struggles is incredibly valuable. Men often feel they have to face challenges alone, but acknowledging that we all need support can be liberating. Working with trauma, grief, and anxiety requires entering these difficult spaces with others, rather than seeing them as problems to be fixed. When someone is willing to enter these spaces with you, it's profoundly impactful, especially in a society where emotional support is often lacking. I've found that people don't want to go through challenges alone. They need someone to walk with them, even if we can't promise safety or solutions. Our role is to be there, offering support and understanding through the process.

Mentoring involves not just guiding others but also learning and growing alongside them. Sharing their own experiences, like navigating challenging times with child support, helps men see they're not alone in their struggles. This approach helps build a supportive community where people feel they can overcome difficulties together. Ultimately, if we can navigate our own challenges and pass on what we've learned, we can ensure that future generations are better equipped to handle their own struggles. The key is to continue using our experiences and insights to support and uplift others, making sure that the lessons we've learned benefit the wider community.

Effecting Positive Change through Mentorships

So much of what we do at DADS is built on embodying and spreading goodness. And, there's a multitude of positive changes we're seeing in people's lives as a result. It took us twenty-five years to get here, but now we can look at individuals like our friend and colleague, Gregory Adams, with immense pride. Gregory, who has been out of prison for more than fifteen years now as of this writing, is someone I am exceptionally proud of, and he plays a crucial role at DADS.

Just this morning, I called Gregory and told him, "You have the most critical role at DADS, I think even more important than mine!" When he finally stopped laughing and asked what I meant, I referred to his role with the Community Corrections Officers (CCOs), previously known as parole officers. Gregory's role involves reaching out to these officers when someone new is coming out of prison. His job is to advocate for these individuals, help them transition back into society, and introduce them to what we're doing at DADS. On this particular call, I gave him the information he needed to go and connect with a new potential client.

Gregory called me back a short time later with some exciting news: the new client he would be working with was a single father, with a six-year-old daughter he hadn't seen since she was two. This father wanted to spend quality time with his daughter, not just brief visits. Immediately, Gregory was on it, working to help find a job for this man and ensure he could secure access to meaningful time with his daughter. Gregory's and other DADS team members' dedication to walking with men like this exemplify the profound impact we're making.

One memorable case was when I overheard a judge's unexpected comment about a young man who was once part of a troubled crew. Despite the man's past, the judge acknowledged his transformation and commitment, which was a testament to the work we're doing. This young man had come into our program, connected with us, and eventually turned his life around. The judge said to him, in front of the whole court, "I know you've changed because I gave you enough time that you could have left and never came back, and yet you keep coming back, so I know you've changed already."

Then the judge turned and said to me, "Whatever you're doing, keep doing it because you're impacting this young man's life!" *Wow.* That judge's words highlighted how our efforts are genuinely changing lives.

Mentors Help Break the Cycle

I remember when I met my first mentor, a man by the name of William Bell, who was the CEO of Casey Family Programs at the time. I had been chosen to be a recipient of an award that the program awarded for serving the community, called the Ruth Massinga award. This was a pretty big deal for Jeanett and me, because we had just opened up our first office, which meant that not a couple of months earlier we had been running DADS from our own living room.

When we first started DADS, winning awards was not part of our plan, or even something we considered a possibility. All we knew was we were trying our best to use DADS to help other fathers in the community, and we wanted to make an impact. We had no clue that we were on somebody else's radar! Not long after this I was recognized twice more for the impact DADS was having. One of them was an award, presented at an event where the keynote speaker was William Bell, which was how I met him.

The other time was when a board member of Casey Family Programs invited me to go to Washington DC and give a testimony up on Capitol Hill. Those were life-changing moments for me. I had always wondered what it would be like to be in a setting like that; not only was I receiving opportunities to meet these important people, but I was presenting to them! Mr. Bell really took a liking to me and what we were doing and he took me under his wing. He taught me more than I can recount and helped guide me as I was still finding my place as a founder and community leader.

For example, I had an employee who was our front-desk receptionist, and at one point I couldn't pay her; I didn't have any money. Back then, William, Jeanett, and I would meet regularly for breakfast. He always liked scrambled eggs and bacon and grits and we called the meeting our "soul food breakfast." That particular day, Jeanett and I were telling him what we were doing and what we wanted to do, but that we didn't have any money.

I said, "I've got to pay this lady. I don't care if I don't get paid but we need to pay her." As soon as we finished telling him about the situation, he placed a phone call and not more than five minutes later he hung up and told us not to worry; he had taken care of it. He was already giving Jeanett and me so much knowledge about working in the community and now this! We were overwhelmed by his generosity and support. We weren't used to this treatment; we still felt like people saw us first as former crackheads. I didn't believe things like this could happen. I had heard about things like this happening, but to *me*, Marvin Charles? That just didn't happen. That was a turning point for me, and a key point in William demonstrating to me, "I'll walk with you." That experience told me it *does* happen to people like me.

Jeanett and I believed that God could use us to help others understand their own value. We knew it had to be people like us to help others from similar backgrounds realize what they were capable of. It was amazing to go up on Capitol Hill in Washington, D.C., and give my testimony. It made me realize that I have a voice and that people are willing to listen, as long as my voice is focused on helping others. It became clear to me that our work must be about uplifting the community, not about lifting up Jeanett and me. The turning point for me was realizing that it's possible and doable. We wanted to preserve the momentum we felt like we gained, so I kept on meeting with William Bell, we moved into the office on Rainier Avenue, and the rest is history.

Breaking the Cycle through Mentoring

Mentoring, especially for Black men, is about breaking the cycle. Many of us didn't grow up with healthy role models, especially when it came to marriage and fatherhood. We may have been taught to be strong, to be tough, to provide, but not necessarily how to be emotionally available or nurturing, to be generous and supportive. For generations, men—and Black men, especially—have been burdened by stereotypes that tell us we have to "man up" and suppress our emotions, and to look out for ourselves first and foremost. But through mentoring, we can learn to unlearn those harmful patterns. We can learn that strength is not about suppressing how we feel, but about showing up, being present, being vulnerable with our families, and being a support and encouragement to those around us.

For men who haven't had positive male figures in their lives, mentoring offers a new blueprint. It's an opportunity to learn what wasn't taught at home, to see up close what it looks like to be a loving father and husband and member of the community. It helps us realize that we're not alone in our struggles—that other men have walked the same path and can offer guidance on how to navigate the challenges. And sometimes, just knowing someone has been where you are and made it through can be the most encouraging thing.

What I've learned over the years is that mentoring isn't just about teaching—it's about walking alongside someone. It's about being available, being consistent, and most importantly, being authentic. The men who mentored me didn't try to present themselves as perfect. They shared their failures as much as their successes, and that was what gave me the confidence to keep going when I stumbled. That's the power of mentorship—it doesn't just give you advice; it gives you someone who's rooting for you, someone who believes in you.

In our community, where so many young men have grown up without fathers or healthy male figures, mentoring is a way to rebuild what's been lost. It's a way to show our sons and nephews what it means to be responsible, loving, and present. And for men who are already fathers and husbands, it's a way to correct the mistakes we've made in the past and become better for the next generation. Mentoring helps us to grow, not just as men, but as leaders in our families and communities.

I've mentored many younger men in my life, and I see it as my responsibility to pass on what I've learned. It's not about having all the answers—it's about being willing to share what I've been through, to listen when they're struggling, and to offer support when they need it. When I see young men stepping into their roles as husbands and fathers, trying to be the best they can be despite not having had examples growing up, I see the future. And that future is bright because mentoring creates a ripple effect. When one man learns to be a better father, and a better husband, he passes that on to his children. He teaches his sons how to treat women, how to be present, and how to love without fear. He shows his daughters what a good man looks like, and what she should expect from her future husband. That's how we change the narrative in our community—one man at a time.

So, to any man reading this who feels like he's missed out on learning how to be a good father or husband, I want to encourage you: seek out a mentor. Find someone who has been where you are and who can help guide you. You don't have to figure it all out on your own. There are men who have walked this road before you and are more than willing to share what they've learned. And if you're in a position to mentor someone else, don't hesitate to step into that role. It doesn't take perfection—it takes a willingness to show up and share your story.

Mentorship has the power to heal, to restore, and to build something new. It's how we learn to be the husbands and fathers our families need, even if we didn't have those examples growing up. It's how we break the cycles of dysfunction and set a new standard for the next generation. I've seen it in my own life, and I've seen it in the lives of the men I've mentored. We need each other to be better, to grow, and to thrive. And it all starts with the simple act of one man reaching out to another.

PASS IT ON

Actively seek out wise mentors and immerse yourself in Scripture to cultivate godly wisdom. Consider whom you could mentor to "pass it on."

He who walks with the wise will become wise,
but the companion of fools will be destroyed.
(Proverbs 13:20)

CHAPTER 5

A Template for Fellowship

Around the same time I was introduced to my first mentor, William Bell, there was a gentleman who contacted Jeanett and said, "We want to give you a grant that is available by invitation only. This is your invitation." So, they gave us a first little piece of grant money. We were so inexperienced that we used the money to put on a banquet, only to find out that if we did that, we wouldn't be allowed to ask for any money! We didn't know that at the time, and went ahead with the banquet, but even in our inexperience, God was good, as you will soon see.

We put down the money to rent the Tukwila Community Center in south Seattle, secured a keynote speaker, and held the banquet. The speaker was the father of a board member who was a colonel in the United States Air Force, more specifically, one of the first African-American colonels ever in the U.S. Armed Forces. Part of what was so fascinating to me about this was that he had been turned down for the promotion nine times before he finally became a colonel. I felt like there was a parallel there: how many times had these fathers who were our clients been turned down too before they actually became "dads"? His tenacity was an inspiration. He didn't give up; neither should the men we serve, as they strive for success in life and parenting.

Anyway, Jeanett and I went ahead with the event with him as our speaker, but then that day it was unseasonably hot outside, and there was no air conditioning in the community center. It became so uncomfortable inside that people started leaving, saying, "Marvin, we love you but we've got to go; it's too warm!" This meant we weren't able to ask for donations at the end because there was hardly anybody left to donate. We only learned later that if we had asked for financial contributions, we would have been breaking the rules of the grant! That was a God-save, for sure!

During that time, Jeanett and I met a young man named Craig Brooke Weiss, who was a champion for fatherhood in our area. We met with Craig a few times, and he came up with a plan to go to the governor of Washington State and present our ideas for combatting fatherlessness in our community.

Governor Gary Locke was in office at that time, and Craig was the one to tell him what was needed from the governor's office, presented our petition, and literally showed him where to "sign on the dotted line." When it was our turn to speak, Jeanett and I shared our story. We told the audience, including Governor Locke, how we had lost our kids to CPS, gone through recovery, and now wanted to dedicate our lives to helping others. This was another pivotal moment for us, telling our story to a room full of important government officials.

Governor Locke said to Craig, "I'm not signing any petition, but if we could figure out how Marvin and Jeanett are doing this,

I'd make it statewide." We were amazed by this acknowledgment. I didn't know it at the time, but there was also a federal government official at the meeting. After it ended, he walked over to me and handed me his business card.

Not long afterward, I received a visit from Levi Fisher, a federal fatherhood advocate who ran the fatherhood division of the ACF, which covered child support, DSHS, and more. I'd heard of Levi, but didn't really know him. One day, he showed up at my house (we were still working out of our living room at this point).

After greetings, I offered him a seat and showed him a video of what we were doing, and gave him the rundown on everything that was happening at DADS. He jumped straight to his point and said, "My boss gave you a card and asked you to contact her. Why didn't you?"

I didn't know who his boss was until he jogged my memory of the federal government official who had handed me her business card at our meeting with the governor. Levi explained that his boss liked what we were doing and wanted to help. That was a big moment for us. As it turned out, the government agency was holding a national conference in Seattle and they invited me to be the closing speaker. I was honored and agreed to do it.

At the event, I played our DADS video and spoke about what we do and why we do it. The impact on my family had been significant, and I knew other families could benefit too. After my speech, a lady came up to me in tears and asked to talk. We stepped out onto a side deck at the Sheraton Hotel, and she told me she wanted to write me a check for five hundred dollars. That had never happened to me before; it showed me that people saw the value in what we were doing.

A month later, Levi came to me and said, "Marvin, Dr. Horn is coming to town and will stop by your office." I was blown away! Dr. Wade Horn was the first president of the National Fatherhood Initiative (NFI) and worked on the administration of both George H.W. and George W. Bush. The NFI had paid for Levi and me to attend a conference in Washington, D.C., where I was a speaker in one of Dr. Horn's workshops about child support and its impact on communities of color.

While I was there, Dr. Horn mentioned to me he would be in Seattle, so I ran down the hallway to catch him and said, "When you're in Seattle, I would love for you to visit our humble office." By that time, we had secured our office. He told me to give my information to his assistant, and he would get back to me. I doubted I would hear from him but now, just four months later, Dr. Horn was coming to Seattle for a fundraiser for George W. Bush and was coming to visit us!

That day, we had community members and folks we had worked with in the room, all listening to him. I was amazed at the turnout. Dr. Horn said, "This is just how the NFI started, in a little room in my house. Then we grew to be doing what we are doing today. Marvin and Jeanett, you are doing great work in the community. The community hasn't woken up to it yet, the country hasn't woken up to it yet, but just keep doing what you're doing!" It was moments like that that gave me an even stronger will and desire to continue.

Later on, Dr. Horn was organizing an event at Chapel Hill and called Jeanett to ask if we could do a workshop. Of course, we agreed. The keynote speaker was Michael Jordan's mother. All evening, Dr. Horn would introduce us as his "dear friends, Marvin and Jeanett Charles, who are doing great work." I never imagined that. It was surreal to hear him, a man who worked with presidents, speak so highly of us and the work we were doing with DADS, despite everything we had done in our pasts.

These experiences showed us that we were making an impact in the community, in the United States, and with the federal government. Anytime someone came to Seattle, they would cut us a check and say, "Dress it up however you want; we're bringing them to your office." This changed us and made a huge difference—all from that first speaking engagement on Capitol Hill and having Dr. William Bell as my mentor.

The Revolution Builds

That's how the national perspective for DADS evolved, but the inner workings within the community really came about in 2006. We had a board member named Mark who often brought a group of kids to the church across the street from our office. At that time, we lived just four blocks from the office.

One of my sons began playing the drums at the church on Thursday nights. My daughters also became involved in the church's summer program, and several young people at the church ended up mentoring my three daughters, teaching them songs and other activities. At the end of the summer, Mark asked us about our fatherhood program. We talked a bit, and he asked if he could visit our office.

One day, he showed up with a check to pay our rent, which we couldn't afford at the time. He even brought enough money for two months. He then invited me to a function the following Saturday, in Yelm, Washington, about an hour south of Seattle, at a Christian camp. I was a bit nervous because I had never been there before. As we drove through the rural area on our way to the camp, we passed a father and son carrying shotguns, which made me uneasy. We asked for directions, and they told us we had gone too far and needed to turn back. Luckily, we made it to the conference without incident.

Once there, I met two men, one of whom was Art Kopicky, who is part of a program called Teleios, of which I am now a member.[3] The environment of this conference was different from what I was accustomed to. I had been involved in Black church ministry, which had a particular way of thinking. This ministry setting was entirely different. We were divided into groups based on the color of our name tags. I ended up in a group with Art, who is now my dearest friend and like a brother to me.

Once we broke into these groups, I realized how much I could learn from these men. The way they spoke to each other, shared what was happening in their lives, and supported one another—it was unlike anything I had ever seen. Where I grew up, a friend was only a friend until they had something to gain by crossing you. So, not just seeing this sort of friendship but being welcomed into it without question was a big deal for me.

---

3. Teleios is Seattle-area men's ministry, founded in 1980, that aims to help men reach spiritual maturity through building bonds of friendship and using small groups, retreats, and service opportunities to foster growth in Christ.

A TEMPLATE FOR FELLOWSHIP

Afterward, Art asked me if I could gather some guys to read the Scriptures together. Not long after that, we started reading the Bible together on Wednesday mornings in our new office.

It was me, five other Black men, and Art. The first thing we talked about was forgiveness. We started reading the Book of Mark. For the other guys and me, it was the first time we could read the Bible and have someone help dissect it for us. We had been to church, but no one had ever done that—asked questions and allowed us to think freely. Usually, you're kind of marched through something and told what to believe, but this was different. There was a whole bunch of great stuff taking place, spiritually.

I don't know if it was Art or the Lord, but one day, someone said, "Do you guys want to go on a mission trip to Mexico to build houses for the poor?"

I was like, "Wow, yeah!" I had always wanted to do a mission trip but could never afford it. Art agreed to take all seven of us.

We planned it, boarded a plane with about twenty-five other men from all walks of life, black and white, and flew to San Diego. We rented two vans and spent three days in Tijuana building houses. The only thing we had to do was give a little bit of our testimony. Everyone had five minutes to share.

After finishing the houses in Tijuana, we drove across the border to Carlsbad, California, where one of the guys had a compound his parents had bought years ago. It was nestled in a little corner, and you could walk across the street to the Pacific Ocean beach. It was amazing.

I was the last one to share my testimony. I talked about what I had been through and where I was at currently. I had been doing small speaking engagements, but the money wasn't good. I had four kids at home, and my wife was a little rattled that I was leaving. I had accepted a speaking engagement that was supposed to pay $3,000, enough to cover our bills. But just before I left, the lady organizing the event called and said the check would be delayed for a couple of months. She hadn't told me that when I agreed to speak. Now I had to leave my family with the rent unpaid. I felt like I was leaving Jeanett in a bind to go off and have fun.

After our sharing time, we all went to get pizza. One of the men on the trip, a senior vice president at Starbucks, said to another guy, "Hey, you know that money I was going to give you? How about I just give it to DADS? It's $5,000." And just like that, the other man agreed, and it was settled. Problem solved.

Before we got on the plane, all thirty-five of us prayed together. In the middle of that group was Connie Jacobsen, the founder of Teleios, who had organized the trip and who subsequently changed my life. That day, he put his arms around me, never letting me go. I learned so much from him.

Connie told me, "I want you to sit on my board. Anything you need to run DADS, you'll find it here." That was a gift straight from God. He said, "I've been wanting to be a part of the urban core ever since 1967. I wanted it so badly that I moved to Chicago to learn what it would take to be able to do something in Seattle, and when I got back, something had changed. It was just before Martin Luther King was assassinated, and the culture had shifted." Connie was a witness to this cultural change, and I was someone who could sit down and explain to him from a Black perspective—how things looked and why.

We talked about Stokely Carmichael, H. Rap Brown, and Huey Newton—young men who were advocating change in the community but who were tired of doing things the way Martin Luther King had done them. They were the upcoming generation, and I was explaining their perspective to him. Connie and I bonded.

It turned out that Connie was Art's mentor—Art, whom I had met at the Yelm conference and with whom I'd been studying the Scriptures and who had invited me on the mission trip to Mexico. The legacy was continuing, and it turned into a circle. I began meeting weekly with Art and Connie. They covered me for everything, offering lifelong lessons. This started to change my understanding, particularly about white folks.

One day, Connie called me. Jeanett and I had recently bought our first house, and these guys were helping me navigate the financial and practical responsibilities (and challenges) that went along with home ownership. Connie was calling because he'd learned from someone else that I couldn't make my second mortgage payment. He said, "Marvin, I thought I was your friend. Friends tell friends when they're in trouble, and I hear you can't make your mortgage payment. As your friend, you should have shared that with me."

He instructed me to swing by his house later that day; he would be away because he needed to take his wife to the doctor's office. He told me there was a milk box on his deck with an envelope inside. He said, "Take that and go about your business." Inside that envelope in the milk box was a check worth enough to cover my next mortgage payment. I was stunned. This one act completely shattered a lifetime of misguided beliefs on friendship.

This is just a snapshot of the process it took to get where I am, but most importantly, I want to point out that it was people like

William Bell, Connie Jacobsen, and Art Kopicky who helped me. They showed me how to get the best out of people by loving them and keeping myself open to them.

Through the years, I have come to understand that fellowship is the living, breathing manifestation of God's love in action. The men who mentored me didn't just preach about love; they embodied it, showing me through their patience, kindness, and unwavering belief in others what true brotherhood looks like. Their example became my blueprint, teaching me that when we open our hearts to others, we invite transformation—not just in them, but in ourselves. In that sacred space of trust and encouragement, I have witnessed men step into their God-given potential, reclaiming their roles as fathers, leaders, and men of integrity.

PASS IT ON

In the face of trials, meeting together strengthens our resolve to persevere in faith, drawing strength from shared experiences, prayer, God's Word, and collective worship.

> *And let us consider how to spur one*
> *another on to love and good deeds.*
> *Let us not neglect meeting together,*
> *as some have made a habit,*
> *but let us encourage one another, and all the*
> *more as you see the Day approaching.*
> (Hebrews 10:24)

CHAPTER 6

Relationship Is Key

My dear friend Johnnie's journey into fatherhood was far from conventional, but he didn't let that stop him from striving to become the best father and grandfather he could. Now in his seventies, he reflects on the many missteps and hurdles he faced as a father and the ongoing struggle to become better for his son. There was no manual on how to be a father, and for Johnnie, that absence of guidance felt like a guarantee of failure.

His past with his own father and the circumstances surrounding his son's upbringing only added to the complexity. Johnnie and his son's mother had known each other since childhood, growing up in a rough environment where her mother's home was a notorious spot for drug activity. Their relationship, and their son, remained a secret for many years to avoid the complications of child support and other legal hurdles.

As his son grew older, though, he knew Johnnie was his father. Still, they kept their relationship under wraps. The secrecy weighed on Johnnie, especially as his son began to mirror him in ways that were hard to ignore. There was one vivid memory Johnnie could never shake—a moment when his son, at around twelve years old, was doing flips outside while hanging around the same dope house Johnnie had once frequented. Watching him flip off a truck, Johnnie was struck by the resemblance; observing his son was like peering back in time and seeing his twin brother as a kid all over again. In that moment, Johnnie felt the undeniable pull of blood, a deep connection to his son. But despite that, he worried—worried that if he stepped into his son's life, his son would end up like him, a failure in his eyes. The fear of repeating the past was paralyzing.

Yet, as Johnnie worked through his own challenges and began treatment for his addictions, he realized he couldn't just leave his son to navigate the chaos of that environment alone. He was attending a recovery program when he mentioned his son's situation to the staff. Their response was direct: "Well, go get him!"

Johnnie hadn't considered such a simple yet profound action—just going to get his son. So he did. While he was at the dope house to retrieve his son, he made sure to check in with the son's mother to clear it with her first. She replied, "Sure, take that one too while you're at it," and gestured to another child in the room, her daughter from a different relationship. So, Johnnie did that too; he packed up his son and this girl who was not his own, and he removed them from the drug house and drove them to the treatment center. It was the first time his son had ever stayed with him, and Johnnie was completely overwhelmed.

He panicked. The enormity of what it meant to be a father hit him like a freight train, and he was unsure of where to begin. That night, he found himself frozen with uncertainty. What did fathers and sons talk about? Should he bring up sports, ask about school, or keep things light? Johnnie had no idea. But even though he didn't have all the answers that night, he slowly started piecing things together. He reached out to a friend, confessing his struggles in trying to relate to his son, and the advice he received was a game-changer. His friend told him, "Kids just want to know you love them, and they spell love T-I-M-E."

That simple truth resonated with Johnnie. He realized that it wasn't about having the right words or perfect activities—it was about being present. The most important thing was showing up, being there for his son, no matter what. Slowly, Johnnie began to embrace that mindset. He got them an apartment—a more stable and secure environment. Still, Johnnie couldn't shake the feeling of inadequacy as a father. He noticed his son engaging in risky behaviors—not the kind that would get him into serious legal trouble, but things that worried Johnnie all the same. He'd come home smelling of cigarettes and weed, and his late-night comings and goings on school nights raised red flags.

Johnnie struggled with how to confront these issues. How could he judge his son when he had made so many mistakes himself? Who was he to tell his son to stay in school when he hadn't always been there to guide him in the first place? The guilt weighed heavily on Johnnie's shoulders. He carried the burden of his past mistakes, unsure how to move forward without being a hypocrite. That guilt reached a breaking point when his son asked to have a serious conversation.

Those words—"a serious conversation"—terrified Johnnie. They carried the potential for judgment and resentment, and Johnnie braced himself for the worst. His son opened up about the struggles he had faced, revealing that he had been abused while living in the dope house during Johnnie's years of addiction. Hearing those words shattered Johnnie's heart. He felt an overwhelming sense of guilt and sorrow for what his son had endured in his absence.

In that moment, Johnnie knew he had to face the truth. He apologized to his son for not being there, for not stepping up as a father when his son needed him most. But to his surprise, his son didn't respond with anger or condemnation. Instead, he told Johnnie that he understood what his father had been going through back then. That conversation, as painful as it was, brought a sense of healing. It was a turning point for both father and son, allowing them to acknowledge the past and begin to move forward. His son's forgiveness helped Johnnie forgive himself—a critical step in his journey of becoming a better father.

Johnnie's advice to other fathers is simple but profound: Don't run from your past. Own it. The mistakes we make don't define us, but how we choose to deal with them does. By acknowledging the wrongs and being open about them, healing can happen. Now, Johnnie proudly calls his son his best friend, and is an eager grandfather to three grandsons and a granddaughter, fully embracing his role in their lives. He knows that being present and showing love through time and attention is what truly matters. It's a lesson he learned the hard way, but one he's committed to passing on.

The Balancing Act

A friend of mine once told me—as his wife once told him—"Make sure that while you're trying to save the world's kids that you don't lose your own." At the time, I thought that it sounded good and all but felt it was a sentiment that didn't apply to me. After all, the guy she was referring to was working at YoungLife; the stakes, in my mind, weren't the same as what we were doing with DADS. These men we helped were at risk of falling back into drugs or prison and losing everything. The cost for me to waver, or take a step back, was too high. Especially as someone who had walked that path already, I knew how necessary our role was.

On top of all that, my children loved DADS. Or at least they had, for a time—a distinction I hadn't come to realize at this point. When we first started DADS, everything was new and exciting for the whole family. Not only were we back together as a family, but we helped other people know that peace too. And with us running the whole organization right out of our home, the kids were involved and felt like they were a part of it. That all changed when we outgrew our little home office and moved into our first official office space. This was a tremendous accomplishment for us, and it felt like it really validated our efforts and solidified our place as a legitimate organization with the resources to make an impact. Unfortunately, the move also severed the connection between my kids and DADS and meant that I was now commuting back and forth instead of working from home. All of a sudden, my time at DADS was time away from my kids, a fact they were acutely aware of.

My children began to see DADS solely in terms of how much it occupied my time. They felt like they were in competition for my attention, and weren't pleased with the results. Our schedules were all becoming busier in unison. They were growing older and joining sports and participating in activities they wanted me to be a part of, and DADS was growing faster than ever and the scope of my responsibilities as founder were growing with it.

At the time, I was just trying my best. I was working to provide for them, I was listening to the Lord, and I was reuniting families.

When my kids first voiced their discontent, I couldn't understand how that wasn't enough for them. How could my kids hate DADS? The job that provided for them? The calling the Lord gave me? The organization that returned fathers to their own friends' lives? The simple answer was—just as Johnnie learned—T-I-M-E. I thought that by getting my kids back, and providing for them, and helping other men to do the same, I was checking all the boxes and then some. I didn't realize how much time I was spending away from them, and how much it affected them.

I'll probably spend the rest of my life answering for missteps in parenting I have made over the years, but I do learn. Little by little I am repairing chips in the mortar of the relationships I have built with each of my children. And now, twenty-six years since I first founded DADS, my last kid still at home has a completely different relationship with DADS than her older siblings did. There are so many facets to every relationship, and they grow and change and evolve over time, often more quickly than our awareness of them does.

This balancing act between our responsibilities and relationships is a universal hurdle for parents from all walks of life, though it manifests just a little differently for everyone. Whether you work away from home, stay home with your kids full time, or fall somewhere in between, there is always something vying for our attention. It is one of those lessons that seems obvious in hindsight, but for so many fathers out there, they've never seen it modeled, or even experienced the other side of it. They might not even know how to talk to their kids, let alone how to best balance the demands on their time to ensure their children's emotional needs are met.

The Diverse Faces of Father Absence

When children grow up without one of their parents, and with no positive role model in that parent's place, they are deprived not just of a relationship, but of a lifetime of modeled behaviors and loving affirmation. These are crucial elements in the development of all children, and their absence can leave lingering wounds that last into adulthood. Learning to bridge the gaps left in our lives by an absent parent is one of the central struggles we help men navigate at DADS. For some, that gap is in knowledge, and they need a mentor to guide them in navigating these unfamiliar waters. For others, the gap is felt more as a sense of longing for that missing connection.

The absence of a father leaves a hollow space in the heart of a child—a longing for something they cannot name, a void they will spend years trying to fill. Too often, that search leads them down dangerous paths, seeking validation in the streets, in unhealthy relationships, or in choices that only deepen their pain. The simple act of a father spending time with his child—listening, laughing, being present—can break that cycle before it begins. But for men who grew up without fathers themselves, this is unfamiliar territory. How do you give what you've never received? This is where the real work begins—learning, through faith and community, what it means to be a father, to show love not just in words but in presence. A man who chooses to invest in his children, even when he wasn't given that example, is rewriting the story for generations to come. That choice—to step in, to show up, to love—has the power to change everything.

PASS IT ON

Acts of service, words of encouragement, and genuine interest in others' well-being are practical ways to live out the life of Jesus in us. Consider how you can actively demonstrate love and honor in your daily interactions.

Be devoted to one another in brotherly love.
Outdo yourselves in honoring one another.
(Romans 12:10)

CHAPTER 7

Mitigating Risk Factors

Years ago, Johnnie and the organization he was involved with worked alongside his city commission, engaging in months of discussions to define what it truly meant for a young person to be labeled "high-risk" or "at-risk." Initially, these terms seemed to suggest something inherent about the child—some flaw or predisposition that made them more vulnerable. But over time, through conversations with social workers, educators, and community leaders, they began to understand that risk wasn't solely about the individual—it was about the world they were growing up in.

Consider Little Marvin. Each morning, he wakes up in a home where his father is getting ready for work, his mother is helping his younger sister prepare for school, and they all gather for a quick breakfast before heading out for the day. As Marvin steps outside to catch the bus, he might walk past a group of men selling weed on the corner or see someone slumped over from addiction. He isn't actively engaging with these things, but just by virtue of his proximity, he is exposed. That exposure, that environment, places him "at risk." The concern isn't just about what he does but about the potential pathways laid before him.

Now, contrast that with a "high-risk" child. Marvin wakes up in a household where his father is in the basement using drugs, his mother has different men coming and going, and his little sister is already experimenting with smoking. Before he even steps out the door, his world is already riddled with instability. In his case, risk isn't just something he passes by on the way to school—it's something he's living in every day.

The key to breaking cycles like these isn't simply telling kids to make better choices; it's about counterbalancing the risks in their environment with protective factors. That might mean ensuring Marvin has access to a strong mentor, an after-school program, or a ride to school that bypasses unsafe areas. Wherever risk exists, we must be intentional about introducing safeguards.

This realization shifted Johnnie's understanding completely—if we want to set children up for success, we must focus not just on their actions but on reshaping the world around them.

Defining and Addressing Risk

That understanding has changed the way I protect my youngest daughter. I try to cover her risk factors by being involved. She and her friends—all in their first year of high school—are, for the most part, low-risk kids. They go out for Christmas dinners together, they plan activities. But I also watch carefully who they let into their circle. For example, there's a new girl they have started to include, and I happen to know her father. We've all done things together, the girls play basketball together, and they've traveled for games. That's a form of support; they understand what it looks like. And where some girls in the group may not have that support at home, the group dynamic helps balance things out. It's all about managing risk by covering each other.

Whom kids associate with is one of the biggest determinants of their future. You want to see where your child is headed? Look at whom they're hanging out with. That snapshot of their friends will tell you a lot. Anytime we can, we try to put our kids in environments where they're not exposed to drugs or risky behavior.

It's easier now than it was with my older kids. These kids have positive outlets—sports, community projects—and they spend their time around other motivated peers. Just recently, my daughter came to me and said, "Dad, I think I want to go to college. Maybe in Los Angeles." We talked about it, and I started a college fund for her. I want her to be involved in that process, so I'm taking her to meet a financial advisor.

No one did that for me or for my older kids, but that's part of my own growth process. We are realizing that, if we want to change the narrative, we need to have these conversations and teach topics like financial literacy, among other crucial topics.

Recognizing and Breaking Cycles of Risk

For Johnnie, fatherhood became a journey of learning the right steps, something he admitted he hadn't known at first. When he started, he didn't always know what to say or do. In the beginning, he simply tried to be the best friend to his son that he could be. Over time, his experiences and conversations with his own son started to make more sense, especially as he watched him raise his grandchildren.

One of his grandsons, Yadi, was graduating from high school as the top of his class and heading to college. Johnnie recalled a conversation where he'd encouraged Yadi to treat school like a full-time job, promising to cover any essentials like phones and shoes, so long as Yadi focused on his education. His son—the boy's father—reinforced the same message, and Yadi thrived with this support.

But another grandson took a different path. Caught up in risky behaviors with a group of friends, Michael ended up in trouble with the law. Johnnie never saw it coming. The boys drove around with a pellet gun, firing it at people from the car. Michael was the one holding the gun that day, and there were serious consequences. Reflecting on this, Johnnie saw how, over time, one child had experienced steady support and guidance, while the other had followed a crowd that led him astray. His son had learned from Johnnie's mistakes, staying closely involved with his own children and working to protect them from similar influences, but one of the sons chose not to engage with the support offered to him

Watching his grandchildren grow into men prompted Johnnie to reflect on his own upbringing. While he had a stepfather during his later teens, no one had ever taught him about finances or other logistical life skills. People just assumed he'd figure things out on his own if he worked hard enough. Instead, he had spent much of his youth searching in vain for worldly fixes to the wound in his heart.

Now seventy years old, Johnnie acknowledges it took him a long time to understand how he got so far off track. Many of his childhood friends had stable, steady jobs and grew into family life, while he had spent years struggling with addiction and instability, living out of hotels, and leading a nomadic lifestyle. They had known something he hadn't—how to work hard, save, and build a life. These skills had never been modeled for him, and worse, his attempts to replace the missing influences in his life had led him to drugs. This is the difference environmental risk factors can make in the trajectory of a child's life.

Once he got clean, Johnnie committed himself to breaking that cycle. Conversations about life, work, and finances became central to his relationship with his son and grandchildren. Some of the talks he has now with his son are lessons he hopes will be passed down to his grandsons. Johnnie has seen firsthand how his son's successes as a father are because he was literally learning from Johnnie's own mistakes and creating a new path for his children by avoiding the same pitfalls that Johnnie fell into.

Every family is unique and faces its own set of challenges. Despite these differences, coming together as a community to lend a hand or an ear helps fill the gaps that at-risk kids can fall through. Johnnie likens it to a "community punch bowl," where everyone can share their insights and experiences. Sometimes you will find kindred hearts in places you wouldn't expect, and other times the simple act of speaking and being heard is a medicine all on its own. The important part is coming together and strengthening the ties of community through communication and trust. An environment of care and consideration is poison to risk factors.

Risky behaviors take on many forms—they look different from one person to the next, yet they all share similar consequences. What might seem risky for one person could be completely normal for another, and knowing what is good for a person often requires insight from those around them. In at risk environments, the only people who might be able to recognize when a child is straying beyond healthy boundaries are often not paying enough attention to do so. By bringing more people to the proverbial punch bowl, you increase visibility of people in the community who may be at risk. This is a strategy for breaking cycles of risk without relying on people who are still trapped in the cycle as the only ones looking for risky behavior.

Recognizing and Redirecting Risk

When it comes to risky behaviors, I've learned to recognize the signs early—both as a parent and as a mentor. Whether it's a newly reunited father or a child exhibiting concerning behaviors, staying connected is crucial. Building strong relationships and reinforcing community bonds are some of the most effective ways to support those at risk and guide them toward better choices.

Risky behaviors aren't always obvious. While smoking, drinking, or petty crime stand out, risks can also emerge in subtler ways—like neglecting responsibilities or failing to keep promises to your kids. Reconnecting fathers with their families is an incredible step, but the journey doesn't end there. The risk of backsliding remains.

Though less common because of the work we do at DADS, I've seen men revert to old habits even after regaining custody of their children. It often starts small, just as my own descent into drug use did—missed commitments, a little dishonesty, cutting corners. Recognizing these patterns early is key to preventing a return to destructive behaviors. With over twenty-five years of experience at DADS, I've witnessed firsthand how risks creep in, sometimes in ways that are easy to overlook.

MITIGATING RISK FACTORS

Raising my daughter, Jamie, has given me new insight into how young people encounter risk. High school comes with exposure to peer pressure, social conflicts, and temptations. While she has always been responsible and level-headed, I constantly ask myself what I can do as a father to help her stay on the right path. I'm not necessarily worried about her experimenting with drugs or making reckless choices now, but I know how easily small risks can escalate. I've seen it happen. That's why I try to be proactive in guiding her toward sound decisions.

There's an old saying: "If you give kids enough to do, they'll be too busy to get into trouble." I've found this to be true, but with an important addition—it's not just about keeping them busy; it's about giving them responsibility and a sense of control over their own lives.

When Jamie turned fifteen, Jeanett and I wanted her to start thinking about the future. We assigned her regular chores, like taking out the garbage and doing the dishes—not just to help around the house, but to instill accountability. However, I knew it couldn't just be about household tasks. To keep her engaged, I also involved her in our family budgeting process, letting her help decide how we allocated a portion of our household income. This served two purposes: it taught her financial responsibility, and it reinforced that her voice matters in our home.

Many teenagers feel caught between childhood and adulthood, struggling to find where they belong. Some turn to risky behaviors as a way to assert independence. By giving Jamie a "seat at the table," I help her transition into adulthood with guidance, rather than letting her seek autonomy in unhealthy ways. With my older children, I took a more hands-off approach, and in hindsight, I see the missed opportunities to provide structure and involvement.

Learning from Real-Life Situations

A recent experience at Jamie's birthday party reinforced the importance of recognizing risk in social circles. She had invited about a dozen friends to a restaurant at the mall. Everything was going well until an argument erupted over social media, leading to a confrontation. Jamie left her own party to go face someone in person, and the situation quickly escalated. Luckily, no one was hurt, but I noticed a pattern—every time I heard this one new friend's name, drama followed.

I pulled Jamie aside and asked, "Why do you keep this person around if trouble always follows?" She defended her friend, saying the drama wasn't her fault. I reminded her that even if she wasn't directly involved, her association with this person could affect how others saw her. More importantly, I wanted her to understand the risks—not just of social conflicts but of being in unsafe environments.

After the incident, one of Jamie's other friends, a girl I respect, came up to me and said, "Mr. Charles, this wasn't Jamie's fault; she had nothing to do with it." I listened and appreciated her honesty. But rather than just letting it go, I took the opportunity to teach them all something. I said, "Every time this girl's name comes up, there's trouble. Why do you keep inviting her without setting boundaries? You should tell her, 'We want you to come, but if you bring drama, please don't.'"

This moment reminded me of something powerful—peer pressure doesn't have to be negative. Just as bad influences can lead kids down the wrong path, good friends can keep each other accountable. Sometimes, teenagers don't want to hear advice from adults, but they will listen to their peers. If they learn to set boundaries and hold each other to higher standards, they can positively shape their own environments.

The Role of Community in Reducing Risk

Risky behaviors look different for everyone and are often shaped by the environment. When I was younger, I had a friend named Darnell whose family was deeply involved in unhealthy behaviors—smoking, run-ins with the law, and a general disregard for consequences. To him, these things were normal. I wasn't engaging in those behaviors myself at first, but by spending time around him, they started to seem normal to me, too. Exposure shapes perception, and that's what I want Jamie to understand.

The same principle applies to the fathers we work with at DADS. Many of these men come from backgrounds where risk was a part of daily life. They've spent years surrounded by behaviors that put them and their families in danger. But just as a risky environment can normalize destructive habits, a supportive community can normalize stability, accountability, and growth.

When fathers leave rehab facilities or the correctional system and reenter their children's lives, they need more than just a fresh start—they need support. No one can do it alone. Parents, extended family, teachers, coaches, and peers all play a role in guiding children away from risk. The same is true for the men at DADS. The best way to mitigate risk isn't just by eliminating bad influences but by surrounding themselves with good ones.

At the end of the day, we can't control every choice our children make. But by creating a strong foundation—both at home and in the community—we can give them the best possible chance at making the right ones.

> ### PASS IT ON
>
> In daily life, being aware of potential risks and planning accordingly is a practical application of wisdom. It involves being proactive rather than reactive.
>
> *The prudent see danger and take cover,*
> *but the simple keep going and suffer the consequences.*
> (Proverbs 22:3)

CHAPTER 8

The Power of Community

For me, community isn't just about friendships or family ties—it's about a shared sense of purpose, a network of support that shapes who we are. I got to experience this in a powerful way when I took a trip to Mississippi with my old friend, Pastor Perry Fields. Perry, now in his late eighties, grew up in Sunflower, Mississippi, as one of eleven kids. He had been a regular at our DADS support group on Wednesdays, and over time, we formed a bond. One day, he invited me to visit his hometown, and I knew this was an opportunity I couldn't pass up.

We flew into Memphis, then drove south through Jackson to Sunflower, where I had the honor of meeting another elder, John Perkins—a man who had been deeply involved in Dr. King's movement. Sitting with these men, listening to their stories, I realized I was absorbing something you can't find in books. Their wisdom wasn't just history—it was a living blueprint for how communities thrive when generations invest in each other. That trip planted a vision in me: I wanted to create a space where African-American youth and elders could connect, share, and grow together.

But it wasn't just the Black elders who shaped my understanding of community. I was lucky to know white men like Connie Jacobsen and Art Kopicky, who defied expectations and crossed perceived cultural lines to invest in me. Connie, in particular, showed me what real friendship means—showing up, no hesitation, when someone is in need. These men helped me understand that building a strong community isn't about focusing on differences; it's about embracing the values that unite us.

That understanding deepened on another trip to Mississippi, this time with three white men and two Black men from our group. Together, we stood on the balcony of the Lorraine Motel, where Dr. King was assassinated. It was a profound moment. Standing there, I could feel the weight of history—but also the reality of Dr. King's dream. He had spoken of a time when Black and white children would walk together as friends, and in that moment, I saw that vision reflected in our own small way. It was a reminder that community is something we build, step by step, relationship by relationship. That vision has been at the heart of DADS ever since.

Building a Spiritual, Cross-Cultural Community

One day, we were doing work with some high school students in South Seattle, and one of the young men mentioned he had never even shaken hands with a white man before. That hit me, and right then, I took him and introduced him to a white friend of mine, inviting them to shake hands and talk. I wanted to create a space where these kinds of boundaries would naturally dissolve—a place where people could connect beyond race or background, just as people.

In our Wednesday morning Bible study group, known informally as "park bench to Park Avenue," we bring together men from all walks of life—those just out of prison and those with privileged backgrounds, like Derrick and Steve, whom I told you about in chapter two. Here, everyone shares their stories, and they do it without blame or resentment. It's about listening, learning, and healing together. This is the DADS community—a place where we focus on understanding and support. It is here, most importantly, that men discover they are not alone. As we read through and discuss the Scriptures together, they learn that Jesus is with them and has given them brothers who want to stand behind them in friendship and prayer.

Though the processes through which we guide these men are very practical and often technical—ranging from parenting classes to legal navigation—we have come to learn that *everything is spiritual*. Beneath the surface of court orders, custody battles, and child support issues lies a deeper, often unseen conflict that shapes the course of a man's transformation.

In the New Testament Scriptures, the Apostle Paul reminds us that our real struggle is "not against flesh and blood but against the spiritual forces of evil in the heavenly realms" (Ephesians 6:11–18). This perspective has become foundational in our work.

It's not just about behavior modification or compliance with systems; it's about healing the soul, restoring identity, and rekindling purpose in the hearts of fathers. That's why we named our organization "DIVINE Alternatives for Dads Services." The name reflects our belief that lasting change cannot be achieved by human effort alone. Divine intervention is not a side note—it's the core of what we do. We believe that every father, no matter how broken or estranged, is part of a bigger story being written by a higher hand.

I was facing a situation when I was 43 years old that could not be overcome by my own willpower, or my own wisdom—it took God. That's when I came to know Jesus Christ, and when He began to begin to set me free and put me on a path that was no longer digging myself into a hopeless pit. Now I lead other men in repeating their own version of my story. For me, it isn't just a one-time event that happened so many years ago; it is an ongoing story, an ongoing struggle, and a commitment to continue to walk and learn with them. I am on the same path they are and I understand the battle, because I am in it every day with them.

The Wednesday Bible study has been going for twenty-five years now. It is a simple formula: just men, Scripture, and open communication. And, in those years, we haven't strayed from the original vision Art gave me. Hundreds of different men have sat in on these Bible studies, men from all different walks of life, and they all have opened their hearts and humbled themselves before the Scripture because Art saw an opportunity to forge a personal connection and share his wisdom. This was God using us to infiltrate the Black community and spread the gospel and mend hearts and relationships.

In and throughout the ministry of DADS, we emphasize the importance of having a *personal* relationship with Christ. In the African-American culture, a history of churchgoing among men is common but a *personal* relationship is not. When they are exposed to men around the circle reading the Bible and sharing life together, they realize that followers of Jesus are not just a bunch of "Bible thumpers." They also can see a difference between some of their past church experiences (where it was all about a show, wearing a mask, or putting on a performance) and what we are doing together. That kind of church experience has turned many men off and they have equated a relationship with Jesus with being religious, saying one thing on Sunday but living another way the rest of the week. This is a paradigm shift that often ends up radically transforming not only a man, but also an entire family.

The men who come to DADS aren't looking to one-up each other or pretend they have it all together; they come to share their truths, support each other, and be in genuine community. It's about creating a space where everyone, regardless of their past or background, can come together to build something positive and lasting. And that, to me, is what the DADS community is all about. When a man comes through our doors, it almost always means two things: he is a father, and he wants to do better. Those two things alone are a strong enough identity that there is never any problem finding common ground between the men in the DADS community. Everything else about that man is secondary to the shared identity of being a father just trying to do right by his children.

There is more to it of course; many if not most of these men didn't have relationships with their own fathers, or are coming out of prison, or recovering from addiction, or all of the above. But, at a heart level, they are men who have recognized they need help, and by coming to DADS, they receive that help themselves and provide it for one another through the power of community.

Building Community for the Next Generation

When we first started DADS, many of the families we were trying to bring together were people we already knew. Some of them were our friends, or people we knew from our old lives, and some of them were the parents of our children's friends. We didn't know it at the time, but we were actively trying to build a community for our kids. By bringing fathers back into the fold, we strengthened not just their own family but the communities they were a part of, which were often the very communities our children grew up in.

I can remember times where one of my kids would come to me and say, "Can you help 'so-and-so's' dad?" They saw the hurt in their friends' hearts, pain they knew all-too-well themselves, and came to me to ask if I could help restore the fathers of their friends at school.

It was encouraging to know my children thought so highly of what I was doing and my ability to reach others, but at the same time it crushed me to realize that, despite breaking the cycle within my own family, there was no way to entirely cut off the impact that fatherlessness would have on the lives of my kids. They had been born into it, and were rescued from it, but were still surrounded by it.

Having escaped a life of drugs ourselves, Jeanett and I were committed to doing right by our children and making sure they knew better lives than we did, but we quickly realized that just turning our own lives around wasn't enough. If we really wanted our children to thrive, the community needed to heal, and we had to do more than just provide an example.

A lot of time has passed since those early days, and while the problems haven't gone away, I've noticed a shift in the way the younger generation of men interacts with fatherhood. It used to be that it was a struggle just to get men to realize they were valuable and necessary parts of a family. Now it is almost shocking how well this next generation is applying themselves to the curriculum of DADS. Even in the face of adversity, there is an enthusiasm to the younger fathers of today that would never have been accepted in my time. And I think this is one of the fruits born of decades of work on behalf of DADS and other organizations to restore not only fathers to their families, but to restore fatherhood, as a concept, to communities for generations to come.

Community Brings New Opportunities

At DADS, one of the key ways we support men in connecting with the community is through our thirteen-week parenting class, focused on what it takes to become an engaged and effective father (see chapter three). Each session is comprised of a group of just over a dozen men, and when one cycle finishes, we start the next. At the end of the thirteen weeks, we rent out the Langston Hughes Performing Arts Center for the graduation ceremony—a small but well-known venue in the community, and a meaningful spot for me because it's where I received my high school diploma.

Many of the men we work with haven't experienced walking in a graduation, so we give them that chance. They put on a cap and gown, and we celebrate their journey. We believe DADS creates opportunities that truly resonate in the spirit. These fathers aren't just graduating from a course—they're taking a step into fatherhood, equipped with tools and support. The course isn't about what they did or didn't do in the past or what their fathers did; it's about making fatherhood relevant for who they are today.

Most of the men who come to DADS want to change the narrative of fatherhood for themselves. Many of them come in "limping," as I say. By that, I mean they're dealing with obstacles—they're disconnected from their children, they're facing challenges with their children's mothers, they're dealing with child support and court orders. These roadblocks can grow into permanent mind blocks if they're not addressed. We use our own stories as examples to help men see what's possible, to encourage them and show them there is a way forward.

In one of our recent classes, we had eighteen men graduating from the program at the same time. I wouldn't have believed it was possible at the beginning, but now, every graduation is a powerful moment for the men, their families, and the community. They invite their family members and share this milestone with them. Our team works together to make each graduation a meaningful experience, and over the last six years, we've seen it grow and take on a life of its own.

This course helps fill in gaps in life and parenting skills that many of these men previously were not aware of, because they were never modeled. And, by not only giving these dads the tools to pick up the proverbial torch where it had been dropped before, but also inviting the community in to witness them graduate, we legitimize them as fathers both in their own minds and in the eyes of their peers, their partners, and the system.

Having parental rights restored is largely a matter of presentation; the people who make those decisions can only assess based on how ready (or not) they perceive a father to be.

Recently we had a man come through our doors, and we walked with him as he fought for a role in his children's lives. He was doing everything he could, taking all the right steps, but still he wasn't making progress within the system, and it was frustrating him. After speaking with him for a while, something finally clicked for me and I asked him where he lived, and he replied, "Around the corner. With my dad."

I said, "No wonder they won't listen to you in court! Get a place of your own so they know you're serious about your kids." It may seem like a minor distinction; a safe home is a safe home after all, and this man was working hard to stay straight and provide support for his kids, but as soon as he moved out of his dad's placed and secured his own, the mom sent the kids to him. He had been putting in the work and was prepared, but he needed more proof, more evidence that he was ready.

The graduation ceremonies for our fatherhood courses instill a great deal of confidence for all parties involved. A man who feels prepared to be a present and involved father is going to appear more prepared, and inviting others in to witness these graduations strengthens the bonds between these men and their communities. The program has led fathers to reconnect with their children and realize they do have a place in their lives. We've seen men who once thought they'd lost their chance to be fathers now fully embracing that role. Some even bring their kids with them to the graduation, to share their stories.

We believe we're onto something important. We're creating opportunities for these men, and the impact is rippling through the community. But it doesn't stop here. I want this program to impact communities across the country. Are we on the right track? Can we make that vision a reality? We think we can. Our goal is to share our story in a way that will resonate with people everywhere. This journey isn't about race or background—it's about the desire to be a father and the willingness to grow into that role.

Support from the Community

That moment I experienced at the Lorraine Motel in Mississippi wasn't just about history—it was about the present and the future. Standing there, I felt the weight of everything that had come before me, but I also saw the responsibility of what comes next. Community isn't just something we inherit; it's something we have to actively build, nurture, and protect.

I think about the young men who come through DADS, many of whom have never experienced true community before. Some grew up in homes where connection was broken, where fatherhood was absent, and where survival mattered more than belonging. They walk into our meetings unsure of their place in the world, carrying the weight of past mistakes and the fear of repeating them. But the beauty of community is that it offers something powerful—redemption, restoration, and the knowledge that none of us have to do this alone.

Community, when done right, becomes a force that pulls people back from isolation and into something greater than themselves. I've seen it happen over and over again—men who once felt lost now stepping up as fathers, mentors, and leaders in their own right. And that's the cycle we need to keep going. It's not just about what we build today; it's about what we pass down to the next generation.

I once heard someone say, "You don't plant a tree for yourself—you plant it so your grandchildren can sit in its shade." That's how I see community. The work we put in today, the relationships we invest in, and the values we uphold aren't just for us. They're for the sons and daughters watching us, for the fathers who will come after us, and for the neighborhoods that will be shaped by the choices we make now.

So, when I think about the case for community, it's not just an abstract idea. It's a mission. It's a responsibility. It's the understanding that none of us rise alone—and if we truly want to change the trajectory of fatherhood, of families, of entire generations, we have to do it together.

At the end of the day, the strength of a man is not measured by what he can do alone—but by the community he helps to build.

PASS IT ON

Just as iron sharpens iron, the Bible says, believers are called to engage in relationships that foster spiritual growth and accountability. Community is essential for personal development and maintaining a strong faith.

> *As iron sharpens iron, so one man sharpens another .*
> (Proverbs 27:17)

CHAPTER 9

Steps on the Fatherhood Journey

I often ask the men who come to DADS, "When did your fatherhood journey start?" Most of them answer with stories of turning points—when they realized they needed to get clean, when they felt the weight of missing years, or when they made the decision to step up and be present in their children's lives. I listen, and then I tell them something that always makes them pause: "Your fatherhood journey started long before you ever made that choice. It started before your child was born. It even started before you became a man. Your fatherhood journey goes back to your own father—even if he was never there."

At first, some struggle to see it that way. To them, fatherhood is something you actively do, not something that was shaping you all along. But whether we recognize it or not, our earliest experiences—what we received, what we lacked, the lessons passed down to us or withheld—become the foundation for the kind of fathers we are, or the kind we fear becoming. Even the absence of a father teaches something. It leaves a blueprint, whether broken or whole, that influences the way we move through the world.

This is why fatherhood isn't just about showing up today—it's about understanding yesterday. The men who walk through our doors often carry the weight of their past, and for many of them, that past includes pain, anger, or confusion about the man who should have been there but wasn't. Some were raised by strong, present fathers, while others grew up watching their mothers do it all alone. Some swore they'd never be like the dads who abandoned them, only to wake up one day and realize they were repeating the same mistakes.

No matter their story, I remind them that their fatherhood journey isn't just about making up for lost time. It's about breaking cycles, about learning what to carry forward and what to leave behind. It's about reclaiming fatherhood—not just for their children, but for themselves. The truth is, a man doesn't become a father when he has a child—he becomes a father when he chooses to be one.

Forging a Fatherhood Identity

The absence of a father is still a part of someone's relationship with fatherhood. The lack of a father influences us just as surely as a present one, albeit in different ways. For many of the men at DADS, recognizing that they embarked on their fatherhood journey long ago and are still being influenced by their own fathers is a pivotal first step in forging their own identity as a father.

Johnnie, whose story we told earlier, was one such man who thought, because of his own upbringing, that he didn't have a fatherhood journey at all. It took being confronted with the truth by someone he trusted in order to begin to accept the many ways in which he still bore the scars of his father's abuse and neglect toward his family.

Throughout his adult life, Johnnie often thought about how men like himself, who had challenging relationships with their fathers, struggled to understand fatherhood on their own. He has seen firsthand how many fathers who are trying to reconnect with their children end up learning on the go—himself included. First-time fathers often don't know where to begin, especially if they didn't have a present or caring father themselves. So, they act on assumptions, engaging in activities they think a father should, like giving their kids money or teaching them about sports. But Johnnie recognized that real fatherhood went much deeper than these gestures—it was about prioritizing time and communication, something he himself had learned the hard way.

Johnnie realized this as he watched young men like Jeff, who initially came to a support group Johnnie attended, only to drift away. But when Jeff's cousin, who had been in a worse situation, turned his life around after attending the same group, Jeff returned, realizing he needed to make the same commitment. He recognized that his cousin was accomplishing things he had given up on for himself, and that the difference was finding a true community and authentic connection versus going it alone.

This idea of coming together to share fatherhood struggles and triumphs was a revelation for Jeff, just as it had been for Johnnie. He saw how powerful it was for men, especially in the Black community, to have a space where they could talk freely—whether about changing diapers or venting frustrations about their children's mothers. These conversations provide an outlet, showing men that, regardless of their differences, they share the same core desire to be good fathers. This drive transcends race, income, and background.

Confronting Fatherhood Trauma

When I pushed back against Johnnie's claim that he didn't have a fatherhood journey prior to his reunion with his son, he took it to heart and reflected on his own father's role in his life. His father had been an abusive man, a tyrant who had sexually abused Johnnie's sisters and regularly beat his mother.

He'll never forget the day his family split in two. It was Johnnie's first day of school, and he came home eager to share his experiences with his mom, only to see her and his sisters hurriedly climbing into a cab. They were gone, and Johnnie didn't see his mother again for three years. He was left with a father who ruled with cruelty and control.

Johnnie has an identical twin brother, and their father treated them differently. For reasons Johnnie never understood, his father always preferred him, regularly taking him fishing while rejecting and even abusing his twin. This inexplicable favoritism left deep scars on both brothers. While Johnnie struggled to confront these memories throughout his life, his brother turned to substance use to cope. Johnnie now recognizes that these traumatic experiences shaped him profoundly, impacting his ability to connect, commit, and feel grounded as an adult.

Years later, buried memories still occasionally resurface for Johnnie, seemingly out of nowhere. He recounted to me a time when his father took him to a shower area at the brick plant where he worked. Johnnie recalled sitting on a bench as men finished their shifts, an experience he'd long pushed out of his mind. It was an innocuous event, but it was a clear memory of days gone by that bubbled up seemingly from nowhere.

Johnnie realized that he had been repressing his memories of childhood, and acknowledging and confronting his traumas had broken the seal. He could trace the resurgence of these memories back to my questioning him about his "father story," a question that initially seemed to hold little meaning to Johnnie but later revealed layers of trauma he had buried deeply.

This process of reflection showed Johnnie the importance of honesty with himself and with his family. As he watched other men come through the support group, some of them fathers and sons just beginning to reconnect, he felt compelled to encourage them to explore their own stories. To this day, Johnnie is a staunch advocate of the importance of having a place where men can share their journeys without judgment, helping each other become the fathers they aspire to be.

Importance of a Father's Role

I remember another time when a young woman came to us, worried about her partner, who had numerous children and was struggling in his relationship with their son. When the two of them came in with their son, I observed their interaction.

Despite her criticisms, her little boy was clearly very attached to his father, which contradicted her complaints. This revealed a different perspective on the father's role, showing that the child's view of his father was much more positive than she had conveyed. This experience reinforced the idea that children often see their parents in a more positive light than their parents might recognize. It's important for parents to see the good in each other and focus on that, rather than dwelling on negatives.

The question arises: why is it so hard for people to understand the significant role a father plays in a child's life? This issue spans generations and involves deep-seated societal views on masculinity and family roles. A significant part of the challenge lies in expectations and communication within the family. Often, parents have differing expectations for their child but don't discuss or align them together. This lack of alignment can lead to misunderstandings and conflicts.

For instance, I noticed that even in my own family, when my wife and I don't communicate effectively, it impacts our children. It's crucial for fathers to be aware of the legacy they're leaving and how their actions affect their children. Many people, especially those with young children, don't fully grasp this until later. Children often recognize and respond to parental dynamics, sometimes more acutely than the parents themselves.

This is why it's essential to focus on the positive aspects of parenting and work together to create a supportive environment for the child. Understanding these dynamics can help address the broader issues in family and community life, leading to more effective support and development for children.

Preparing Men to Earn A Relationship with Their Kids

If you've made it to the table and asked, "Am I the only one?"—half the work is already done. Now, it might not feel that way, because you're still thinking, *What about this? And what about that?* But sometimes, you've got to clear the slate and take that first step. Understand where you are, and then think about what you need to go forward.

For example, you may be asking, "I'm a father who has lost access to my children. How do I regain that access?" First, clear the slate, so there's space to build. The first step is determining what needs to be done. Many men want to restore their parental rights, but that may not always be possible. That doesn't mean you've lost; it just means you need to establish a relationship with your children, maybe in a different way.

If you're coming off drugs or just out of prison, you might need to start by working on yourself. The first step is re-creating yourself in your own eyes, and in the eyes of the community. You might not realize it, but as you do this, you're building credibility. Now, you have an employer who knows you, a landlord who sees you, other people in the community who witness the work you're putting in. That old stigma starts to disappear, little by little.

If you live in the same community as your kids or their mother, people are watching, kids especially. They may hear from others in the community, "I saw your dad, and he's doing well." Kids might not bring that information home to their mother, but they store it. They hold onto it. Kids often say, "I can't wait until I turn eighteen." That comes from a place of wanting to see things for themselves, not just going by what others tell them.

I encourage fathers to keep going on this journey, even if it's difficult, because one day, that child may come knocking on your door. And when that happens, you don't want the last word to be,

"I couldn't do anything." Instead, you want to show them, "This is what I did."

One of the fathers we worked with went through this journey. After spending five years in prison, he was trying to reconnect with his kids, but their mother was asking for more child support than he could afford. We helped him get settled in a halfway house, found him a landlord willing to give him a chance, and he started working hard, taking whatever jobs he could. Recently, he told me, "I'm finally able to see my boys." He doesn't have full access yet, but he's present in their lives, contributing financially, and they see him regularly.

The mother recently took him back to court for additional child support because one of the boys is going to college. During the hearing, she was on Zoom while he was present in court. He told me afterward, "I did exactly what you told me to do, and it went well." This man, after a five-year journey, is finally seeing the positive effects of his hard work.

I believe that if we work within the system, it can yield favorable results. Now, maybe I'm a little naive, but from what I've seen, fathers who dedicate themselves to the process—who don't fight or argue with the system—tend to find satisfaction and even some success in their fathering journey. It doesn't look the same for everyone, but it's about making progress, step by step.

Ultimately, I believe a father's role is to prepare his children for a future he will never see. By staying engaged, rebuilding credibility, and taking it one step at a time, we can create a foundation where our kids see us as fathers worth listening to. That's what this journey is all about.

PASS IT ON

Consistent teaching and modeling of appropriate behavior by parents and guardians are crucial. This includes not only what we do, but also our worldview, values, and relationship with God. Children learn not only through instruction but also by observing the actions of adults.

*Train up a child in the way he should go,
and when he is old he will not depart from it.*
(Proverbs 22:6)

CHAPTER 10

The Loss of My Father

We are all on a fatherhood journey, and I am no exception. In October of 2023, my own father passed away. I had no idea the impact that this was going to have on my life—not just on me personally, but on my children, my wife, and my family as a whole. It took me months to realize how much I was hurting because I lacked knowledge about my dad. I had questions that now would never be answered because I couldn't talk to him anymore. I would have to settle with what I already knew about him for the rest of my life.

It wasn't one of those situations where you know the end is near and you can spend the last days, weeks, or months connecting and reminiscing. I didn't meet my father until I was already a father myself, and when I finally saw him for the first time, I learned he'd had a stroke that left him with aphasia, which meant he wasn't able to communicate effectively. He could barely talk to me. And that left a void. Here I was, meeting my father for the first time, and I was already too late to get to know him properly.

I was used to having voids in my life that I had to deal with; this was just one more of them. But unbeknownst to me, this would be an opportunity to fill those voids; I just didn't see it coming.

Though I never learned as much about my father as I'd have liked to, most of what I do know I cherish. Affectionately called Wolf by his family and friends, Willie R. Cheatham was born to a single mother in the 1940s. His mother left him with his grandmother, who already had eleven children. So, my father grew up with his uncles and aunties, a few of them younger than him.

My grandmother eventually remarried, and the husband she married suggested she go and retrieve her son from her mother's house and he would adopt him. That's how he became William Cheatham. My father would tell me stories about his stepdad, my grandfather, how he played baseball for the Negro Leagues and was in the military. He told me that when he played catch with his dad, his hand would always hurt afterwards! That was a pretty significant topic whenever I talked with my father, even though it took him forever to have just one conversation. But I do remember how that memory of his stuck out in my mind.

Other than that, I didn't know much about my father. I know he had two other children besides me: one sister six months older than me and another one fifteen years younger. The younger one was named Stacy; the older one was named Kathy. I met his mom—my grandmother—once, a year or two before she passed away. I know my father grew up in Tacoma, Washington, and I know he spent most of his life living in Oakland, California, which is where I met him for the first time in my life.

THE LOSS OF MY FATHER

Meeting My Dad for the First Time

I was a little hesitant in meeting my father for the first time because, when I called him on the phone, he sounded different—the kind of different that I didn't want to see. But I was already in the Bay area and I had his grandchildren with me. They were young at the time, and so one of them asked if we could go back across the Bay Bridge. And I realized then, *Okay, this must be a sign I need to go see my dad.* So I went to see him at his residence, a low-income community of subsidized housing where he rented a small apartment.

When I saw him, I realized immediately there was something medically wrong with him; that's when I learned he'd had a stroke. When I left that meeting, I felt like the door to a relationship with my father had slammed shut. I don't know if I ever expected to see him again. Actually, I wasn't making any plans to go visit again. I just thought, *Okay, I met my dad, check.* I honestly don't think I was interested in creating a relationship with him at that time. I got on my plane and went back to Seattle.

Once I was back home, I told my mom I had visited my dad. Unbeknownst to me, she'd made some plans to go see him herself. Just a few weeks later, my mother was on a plane. She went to see my dad, and he asked her to marry him. She said yes! They rented a car, she loaded up his stuff, and they drove back to Seattle.

At this time in my life, that really didn't seem like a bad idea; it just seemed like an answer to the prayer I had prayed a year or two prior to that: "Lord, help me put my family back together again." And now this thing was unfolding before my very eyes. Jeanett and I had just married earlier that year. So there I was, with my children, my wife, and my parents, all together. There was this family, for the first time in my life—a complete family.

But then the reality set in. My mother and father were married, and they lived in one part of the city. Jeanett and our children and I, we lived in another part of the city. We were all close to one another, doing our own things, and I assumed everything was going great. But one day my mother came to me and said, "You need to work with your father."

I thought, *What does that mean? I need to work with my father?* But she was insistent that they needed my help, and I wasn't prepared for that. I wasn't even thinking about that. I thought the hard part was over when my family was reunited—but that was only part of the equation.

I tried to speak with my father, but it was still very difficult to have a productive conversation with him. And so, within six months, my parents were living in separate locations again. I don't know if any of us really thought that situation out well at the time because the idea of a being a "whole" family was just so exciting to us. My mother passed away a few years later, and then I had to find a place for my father to live. I had to be Mr. Fix-It.

Dealing with Dad

Dad preferred independent living, so, as a dutiful son, I applied myself to arrange all of that. And it worked out well. For the first ten years of our relationship, I catered to his every need in addition to my roles as a husband and a father at the same time. It was difficult, but I did the best I could.

About year fifteen, things started to go a little sideways, but he was still my dad. I'd never had one before, and I felt I needed to be a dutiful son. But as a few more years wore on, some of my father's behaviors caused by his condition began to cause some serious issues. I think that's the best way to say it. For one, the aphasia was causing him to say things that weren't true, and to use profanity. I'd always say, "Dad, you can't cuss around my kids. You can't." I would have him at my house and we'd fix him dinners but when things didn't go his way, he would become belligerent.

So, finally, after nearly two decades of catering to his needs and dealing with his antics, I got to the point where I felt like, *Enough is enough*. At this time, he had a really good caregiver whom I knew pretty well and my father got along with her, but most importantly, she knew how to deal with him, and I was able to entrust her with more of his care. She would call me regularly with updates and tell me what I needed to work on with him. This was a helpful dynamic that decreased the strain of caring for my father and gave me some space to just be a son. I knew he was in good hands with his caretaker. She would keep me up to date on doctors' and hospital visits, and she helped maintain his social credit; she truly went above and beyond for him.

Then everything changed again. I remember receiving the call: "Your father has had to go to the hospital." I spent as much time as I could with him in the hospital, and while he was there, he kept saying "I wanna go home, I wanna go home, I wanna go home." And nobody was really telling him the truth, that he wasn't going to ever go home. He just kept saying he wanted to go home. To placate him, his caregiver told Dad, "In order for you to go home, you have to get better. You've got to eat." But he wasn't eating. He wasn't doing a lot of things.

That's when I placed a call to his younger daughter, my half-sister, and told her what was happening; she promptly flew in from Oakland. I asked, not with the greatest attitude, "Are *you* prepared to take him home?" I was a little frustrated because it had been thirteen years and nobody from Oakland had come up to see him. Nobody else had been a part of his care, and I'd been shouldering all that responsibility. I wanted to know if she was willing to take a turn. That was my mindset.

To my surprise, she responded better than she could have, and said yes. She was willing and able to take him home and care for him. However, his doctors felt differently; they made it very plain to us that he probably was not ever going to be able to go back home again. That's when the reality set in for me.

We left the meeting and my sister looked at Jeanett and me and said, "You guys have done an amazing job." I wasn't expecting that. I thought, *Really?* It was the first time somebody had acknowledged anything good to me about my relationship with my father. I remember feeling, *Wow. I guess I have been all right with him.* Prior to that moment, I had never been validated by my family in my effort to care for my father, not once. Nobody ever gave me any encouragement. People outside the family might have said, "Man, you're a good son." But when people who don't intimately know what's going on say things like that it doesn't have the same significance as those closest to you. My sibling said it and it had a whole different impact.

Other family members started telling me stories about the house my sister lived in, and how it was full of remembrances of my father. She said, "You need to come see." So, here I was, finally starting to develop a connection with my sister, a connection I'd been searching for my whole life. It had been right there all along and I didn't even know it! Eventually she had to return home, of course; but I am forever grateful for her efforts.

Time to Say Goodbye

One morning not long afterward, I received a call from the hospital, saying, "Your father's breathing isn't good; you need to come right away." Jeanett and I got there within twenty minutes, and his breathing was shallow, but he still stood up and was calling my name and saying all sorts of things. They were trying to take his blood and he was shouting, "No, no, no!" Honestly, that was my father's favorite word: "No, no, no, no!" I could feel he was asking for help.

I pulled the doctor and the nurse to the side and said, "Can you just leave him alone, you know? If this is his last ride, then just leave him alone. Don't bother him." Then Jeanett and I took over the final moments of my father's care. We brought in my uncle and we all prayed for Dad. This was his last journey and we wanted to give him peace in it. We just prayed that prayer over him, for God's peace. For a little while, he was peaceful, not trying to get up or shout anymore. A couple of hours later, he passed away.

I remember having the thought, *What better place can the son be but with his father when he takes his last breath?* Out of all the stuff that I've been through in my life, for some reason it was this moment where I felt like I was truly in the right place at the right time. I wasn't expecting that. I didn't see that coming.

Then reality kicked in. *What do we do with Dad's remains? What's the next step?* I had never made end-of-life arrangements before. But if you're going to do it, your dad is whom you should be able to do it for. And so we did.

I called my sisters and told them, "Dad has passed away."

My younger sister said. "Whatever you do, I'll support you." That meant a lot to me. I'd never been honored like that before in my family of origin. You see, I'd always felt I was a father twice and a son once. When I met my dad, I didn't get a chance to be a son. I had to be a father, had to be a caregiver. So, for a long time, I felt robbed. But through this turn of events, I realized I was supposed to be a father twice. God prepared me for this responsibility when He put me on the path to be my father's caretaker.

My sister and I agreed that she would put together the obituary. I set a date for the service. I started building the program, found a church for the service, planned the details with Jeanett's help, and then thirty days later, we had the service. The service was performed by the pastor who helped me baptize my father when he gave his life to Christ.

Yes, my dad gave his life to Christ, which I count as the biggest blessing, and which relates to another thing I know about my father, and I'll forever smile at this fun fact about him. At his church, he was the head of the Mint Ministry. (I'm mostly kidding but a little bit serious). Dad would purchase a case of Altoids and every Sunday would be at church and pass Altoids out to everybody. So, they affectionately called his efforts "Pop Cheatham and the Mint Ministry." When I told my sister that, she bought a case of little bitty Altoid tins and wrapped them up all nice. When she got to the funeral, she passed them out to guests in honor of Pop Cheatham and the Mint Ministry.

Reflections on My Relationship with My Dad

I had a profound realization during that service, something that affects me strongly even now as I am writing this. My father made more memories and connections in the short period of life he spent up in Seattle with my family than in all the many years I missed out on. When people tell stories about their father, they talk about stuff they did when they were growing up. But that was not the case for me.

I never gave that loss any credit or any power. I had just been assuming my father and I came into each other's lives too late to make a significant mark—until the day of his memorial service. Then, I realized that my father *did* make an impact on my life. And that I made an impact on him.

I didn't come to this realization based on what I knew about my father. It was based on some comments my sister made to me. She said, "Our father had a better life here in Seattle with you than he would have ever had in Oakland." That took me aback. I was so wrapped up in the necessity of caring for him that I didn't realize I had been enriching his life by bringing him into mine.

And, beyond that, I had missed the fact that he was proud of me. We determined, after the fact, that he had been proud of me, since he never flat-out said it. I had been looking for him to tell me stories of how he was proud of me, or to provide some other clear-cut sign of his approval, and he couldn't do that. But God used his memorial service to show me how many people my father had connected with despite his aphasia, and how clear it was to all of them how proud he was of me. For example, I would take him to our DADS banquets every year, and he would always say simply, "Marvin, Marvin." And what he was saying to me was he wanted me to introduce him to everybody who was there. He relished being a part of what I was doing.

To my surprise and gratitude, many of those people showed up at his memorial service, and talked and talked about the impact that this man, my father, had in their lives. There were stories after stories about how his few words were empowering to a lot of other people.

This was a new perspective for me, that's given me much pause and food for thought. I honestly don't recall, in my whole life, having to think about my parents in a constructive way. And now I'm realizing my faith journey and my father's journey, they are intertwined. My relationship with my father, and the fatherhood work that I do today, it's all intertwined.

Without him, I wouldn't be the man I am today, and I wouldn't be doing the work I am today. I recognize and embrace all the ways in which my relationship with my father, both the times of presence and of absence, have shaped me and helped me along this path God has charted for me.

PASS IT ON

A righteous life not only honors God but also brings joy to those who have invested in our spiritual growth. Parents find deep satisfaction in seeing their children walk in truth and right living.

> *The father of a righteous man will greatly rejoice,*
> *and he who fathers a wise son will delight in him.*
> (Proverbs 23:24)

CHAPTER 11

The Men of DADS

This fatherhood journey we are all on is more than biology; it is presence, commitment, and love in action. Yet, for many men, life's struggles—addiction, incarceration, systemic barriers— erode their ability to be there for their children. DADS exists to change that. The men who come through our doors don't just find resources; they find a brotherhood, a second chance, and a calling greater than themselves.

It is hard to quantify the impact DADS is having on these men, but we have obtained a few measurements of the services DADS has provided over the years in an attempt to contextualize the work we do.

From 1998 to 2024, DADS served 5,731 fathers as well as their 13,109 children. Since 2021, 58 percent of fathers who have come to DADS reported that they received support with getting visitation with, or custody of, their children. During that same timeframe, four out of every ten fathers who came through our doors returned for subsequent visits. But, for the men who received spiritual guidance or prayer on their first visit, that number is eight out of every ten![4]

---

4. DCYF Prevention Services Application Data. www.thecapacitycollective.org. Accessed April 15, 2025.

Faith is at the center of what we do at DADS. It's in the name, after all, and it's the special sauce that sets us apart from other similar organizations who are trying to repair our communities. Ultimately, the numbers do little to capture the real impact of what we do, which is measured by the lives changed, and the testimonies we hear. That is why we have asked a number of men who have either gone through the DADS program themselves, or who have walked alongside me, to share their stories, so that others can see a glimpse of what is possible through Christ and community.

A Legacy of Fatherhood Restored

I asked a few men who have walked through DADS' doors over the years for permission to share their stories, to give voice to the journey from brokenness to restoration. These are men who have been on—and stayed on—their fatherhood journeys for years, and who have created legacies with far-reaching ripple effects. Their stories aren't just about what DADS has done for them, but about what they have done for their children, their families, and their communities. These are men who have transformed their own lives and, in doing so, have rewritten the legacy of fatherhood for the next generation.

David Johnson: Seizing the Second Chance

In 2003, David Johnson was at a breaking point. Addicted to drugs and alcohol, drowning in child support payments, and unable to hold down a stable job, life felt like an unbearable weight. The state offered no relief, and his hope was running dry. That's when he made the decision that changed everything: he sought treatment.

THE MEN OF DADS

By 2004, David was in recovery, staying sober, and engaging with a church-based program at Union Gospel Mission. It was there that I met him, and was able to share with him how his experience navigating the child support system mirrored my own. But I had had already made it to the other side, and I was willing to help him if he was willing to learn.

David says, in reflecting on those years,

Back before I got clean, I felt like everybody knew each other within the Black community in a way that is lost today. And part of that was I knew Marvin, everyone did, and what he and Jeanett had overcome in reuniting their family. People who were still struggling saw what they had done as an inspiration, and they never shied away from that. They embraced it.

Marvin utilized the connections he had within the community to lift people up and guide them on the path he had walked. He and Jeanett gave their time, their resources, and their belief to anyone within the community who wanted to be better, and the results speak for themselves.

Through Jeanett's and my guidance (Jeanett is an expert when it comes to helping our DADS clients navigate "the system"), David learned how to advocate for himself within the structures and processes laid out for him. He attended classes aimed at strengthening Black men within their families, realizing that his personal healing was essential not just for himself, but for his children. He became part of the brotherhood at DADS, walking alongside other men on the same journey of rediscovery.

As David's life stabilized, he found meaningful work in human services. His nights were spent working, and his days were devoted to his children—attending field trips, cheering at sporting events, and being the father he once believed he could never be. Though he never won full custody, he never let that deter him from showing up. Even when he had to pay child support while his kids stayed under his own roof, he saw it as an investment in their future, not a setback.

Over time, David's career flourished. From an entry-level position to senior director at Plymouth Housing, he climbed every rung of the ladder. He bought a home—an unthinkable milestone, considering his past life. He fully paid off the $37,000 in child support debt he owed, which once felt insurmountable. And above all, he showed his children that transformation was possible.

His nickname for himself became "the Opportunist"—not in a self-serving way, but as a man who seized every opportunity that God placed before him. Today, his children are college-bound, and he stands as living proof that fatherhood is not defined by past mistakes, but by the choice to fight for a better future.

Parris Johnson: The Long Road to Brotherhood

When I first met Parris, somewhere in the years between 1999 and 2001, he wasn't looking for guidance. His mother was a minister at True Vine Holiness Missionary Baptist Church, and he attended her sermons sporadically. One night, as he tried to slip out of church unnoticed, I caught him at the door and spoke words that, he told me later, lingered in his mind: *"The battle for your soul is being fought in heaven right now, and heaven will be victorious."*

At the time, Parris didn't think much of it. But as the years passed, we continued to run into each other—at church, in the community, even crossing paths at a bar, where I had stopped in to greet one of our clients whom I knew was there. Parris knew my character; no explanation was necessary.) But me showing up—even there—was a reminder that God was moving in his life, whether he recognized it or not.

Parris reflects on how our relationship played out:

Through the years, I continued seeing Marvin around—always in the community, always helping, always giving. He was a resource, someone you could always count on. He never judged people for their past mistakes; he just loved them where they were. He saw people, not their failures. That kind of love was hard for me to understand at the time, especially since I grew up without my father. Having a father figure felt unfamiliar, even uncomfortable.

One of the other ministers at the church where I met Marvin had a ministry called "Lace 'Em Up," where groups of married men met on Zoom every first and third Saturday. Marvin was part of that. During one of those calls, Marvin mentioned he and his wife were heading up to Capitol Hill for ice cream and burgers. I told him to stop by my shop. I didn't realize at the time that both he and his wife were into sneakers, so when he came through, we got to talking and grew even closer.

After this point we started talking directly more frequently, and he told me about his journey as a father, as a man of faith, and as the head of DADS. It took me a while to realize it, but it clicked that Marvin wasn't just someone that other people could count on; he was someone that I could count on, a resource I had access to, without question or any strings attached. It was an incredible gift to receive his friendship, and Marvin gave it so freely."

By 2005, Parris had given his life to God. I officiated his wedding that same year, and our bond deepened. Over time, he realized that I wasn't just an impersonal leader of an organization—I was a consistent and caring presence. Whether celebrating milestones or standing in the trenches during struggles, I would be there, for him and for others.

Through DADS, Teleios men's Bible study, and the mentorship of men in both of those groups, Parris built a support system he never knew he needed. When he bought his first house, we were there—literally. Having overheard Parris mentioning his new home, I called the next day, asking what he needed. By the weekend, we and some of our crew from DADS showed up with a U-Haul full of furniture, enough to fill the entire house!

Parris says,

Sometimes, life experiences make it hard to trust, especially if you struggle with isolation, depression, or worry like I do. But having people you can call—not because you need something, just because you need to talk—that's different.

That's what Marvin has been to me—a mentor, a friend, a brother. And I pray that I can be that for someone else.

Through this brotherhood, Parris learned that ministry isn't about sermons—it is about life. At DADS, we don't just preach about community; we try to live it. And in doing so, DADS modeled a new kind of fatherhood for Parris, one that extended beyond blood to every man willing to walk this journey.

Anthony Robinson: Redemption in Action

When I met Anthony Robinson in 2009, he had just been released from prison and was dreaming of starting his own nonprofit. He was introduced to DADS by a mutual acquaintance, and the work we were doing resonated deeply with him. But despite initial enthusiasm, Anthony found himself slipping back into old habits. Addiction pulled him away. That didn't stop us, though; I never stopped checking in.

In 2017, Anthony's life took a dramatic turn. His daughter was born two and a half months premature due to his and her mother's drug use. Months later, he was back in jail. Sitting in his cell, he knew he had to change—not just for himself, but for his baby girl. He wrote to me, unsure of what to expect. I responded simply: *"Sit tight. I'm coming."* And I did.

When I got there, I didn't offer empty promises or feel-good optimism. He needed to take the situation seriously—but that decision was up to him. I asked Anthony a single, powerful question: "What's different this time?"

Anthony knew the answer. For the first time, someone else needed him more than he needed himself. His daughter's fragile life was a call to action he couldn't ignore.

Upon release, Anthony came straight to DADS, following every step we laid out for him. DADS helped him navigate the system, secure visitation rights, and rebuild his life. His visits with his daughter moved to DADS headquarters—a safe, welcoming space where fatherhood could flourish and they could bond. After eight months, he won full custody.

The influence of DADS in Anthony's life extended beyond paperwork and procedures. As his mentor, I tried to validate

Anthony's worth, pulling him into circles of influence, treating him not just as a mentee, but as a brother. When Anthony's sister passed away, his DADS family helped arrange his travel, ensuring he could be there to grieve with his biological family.

Anthony recalls,

> "We got you." That's what Marvin has always said; time and time again, he and DADS have been there to assist. He has supported me not just with provision, but by including me in his life too, asking me for input and validating me in ways that were brand new to me. Marvin's friendship is all encompassing; he never backs away from your problems and he invites you into his circles with no hesitation.
>
> Now, because of Marvin and DADS, I have a family. The three of us are still all together, and my daughter is thriving. I knew, from that moment in my jail cell, that I was willing to do anything to get to this point, but it took the support of community to in order to show me the path and make it a reality.

Today, Anthony is clean, employed, and providing for his family. He has not only reclaimed his role as a father but has stepped into leadership within his community, proving that redemption is possible when coupled with relentless support and personal resolve.

A Legacy to Continue

The work of DADS is not just about helping men become fathers—it's about restoring families, rebuilding communities, and breaking generational cycles. The men who walk through our doors leave not just with tools, but with purpose.

I know that Jeanett and I, as founders, have for a long time been the heart of this movement, but like Moses with Joshua, every leader must pass the mantle. The next generation of DADS leaders will rise—not because of an organization, but because of a brotherhood that refuses to let men fall through the cracks. These stories are proof that fatherhood, no matter how lost it may seem, can always be found again.

PASS IT ON

Through the redeeming power of Christ, broken lives are healed and families are restored. Through Christ, all things are possible!

Therefore, if anyone is in Christ, he is a new creation;
the old has passed away, behold, the new has come.
(2 Corinthians 5:17)

CHAPTER 12

God Will Provide

I recently received a phone call from a gentleman with the Department of Corrections, and he left me an interesting voicemail, "Mr. Charles, I've heard a lot about you. I wonder if we can have a conversation."

So, I called him back and he started telling me what he'd heard about the work I was doing. He worked in a division of the Washington State Department of Corrections called "Strengthening Families," which helps fathers coming out of prison connect to their children. I said, "Well, I'll tell you what; let's set up a meeting." So, he brought his supervisor and another colleague and I showed him what we do at DADS.

I took him on a tour of our office, and, that morning, there just happened to be a Bible study going on at the time. There were two gentlemen in the room and one of them recognized the DOC worker. He exclaimed, "Hey, she used to be my counselor at Shelton!" We entered the room and struck up a conversation.

Seeing one of their previous inmates in a Bible study at DADS must have had an effect on the corrections officials, because the next thing I knew, they were in my office, peppering me with questions. "Listen, we need what you do! How can we funnel the people that are coming out of prison to you?" I was floored at that. The Department of Corrections was coming to me directly to ask for help? I could hardly believe it.

When we started the ministry, more than twenty years ago, Jeanett and I used to go into the halfway houses and sit down and work with the men coming out of prison, because God said that was where He wanted us to be. He told us that if we introduced men to their children, they wouldn't go back to prison. He told us it would be difficult to do that because of all the barriers that were against them, but laid it on our hearts that if we connected the men with their families, they would feel compelled, just like Jeanett and me, to fight for their them.

So, we were going to them—the DOC, the halfway houses, the treatment centers—seeking these men out, handing out pamphlets, putting in the legwork just to get in touch with them, because there were no other systems in place to help these men help themselves. And now, over two decades later, here I had the Department of Corrections coming through our door for help.

That's God right there. What I need He'll bring to my door; I don't have to go searching for it.

Faith and Finance

It took a lot of time for all of this to come together, but for me that was a part of understanding how He operates. We had to strengthen, tighten, and professionalize what we do, and that took time.

This current arrangement that I see as a blessing would not have really worked out in the middle or at the beginning of DADS.

At that time, we hadn't learned where our strengths were and what works and what doesn't. Some people have a mindset of *Hurry up, hurry up, and get this done.* I've learned God has reasons for allowing things to evolve over time because it gives you the ability to make sure what you are doing is right and done right.

So much has changed from the time we were going into the halfway houses to now. The Community Corrections Officers who mind the guys coming in and out of prison can't just come to an organization operating on my kitchen table and ask for a copy of the books and see the materials that we use. But when we were still in that kitchen, I had no idea what God had in store for us. I had to trust the Lord completely, having no idea where he was taking me. I didn't have a clue. All I knew was that He told me, *Don't go looking for anything because what you need I'll bring to your door.* Time and time again He has delivered exactly what we need.

Miraculous Provisions

When we approved our 2024 budget, we thought we were $200,000 in arrears, and at the same time we were transferring treasurers. So now we had an in-house person who was working at it and learning, and I trusted him, but I admit I was nervous. He was new to the position and the numbers weren't looking good even before he started. I found myself worrying about what could happen. And then the $200,000 deficit dropped to only being $10,000, and a massive weight left my shoulders. Praise God!

Now, $10,000 is still a large sum of money and I didn't know where it was going to come from—but where else could it come from but the Lord? Amazingly, we found the source of the missing $10,000 . . . we were owed a check that had been sent to the wrong address!

We contacted the provider of the check, and they were supposed to re-mail it to us before the end of the year. We called them again almost three months later and said, "Hey, we never did see the check."

They replied "Well, somebody cashed it!"

Uh-oh!

But yet again, God came to our rescue. We came to find out that the check had been sent to another DADS account, and had already been cashed, so we actually had the money the whole time!

Once we figured that out, we zeroed out our budget for the year, which was above and beyond what I was expecting just a few months prior.

God always comes through. He always comes through!

The Library: "If You Build It, They (Books) Will Come"

Shortly after moving into our current building, one of our donors from the Geisner Johnson Foundation came and asked us, "So what do you want to do with all of this empty space?" I knew I needed a classroom, a recording space for men to tell their stories, and I knew that I wanted to build a library, so we started to plan it all out.

I had a collection of books that were given to me by two of my mentors, that I planned to use to start the library. My mentors were knowledgeable men, one of them a scholar, and I felt like these books represented all the wisdom they had passed down to me over the years, so I was excited to put the books on display in the library. A company came out and built us our classroom, and the podcast room, and some beautiful bookshelves all the way around the classroom. I added my collection . . . and it barely made a dent in the shelf space! There was still so much room for books it looked almost silly.

A couple of people started giving me grief in a friendly way: "Like, he knows he don't have that many books, right?"

But I trusted God enough to know that He was going to give me whatever I needed. He had been doing that so far and He had made it very plain: "Don't go looking for anything."

Well, then, I received a phone call one day from Child Haven, an agency I had worked with frequently throughout the history of DADS and even prior to that. Before Jeanett and I recovered custody of our children, the state would send them to this therapeutic practice for kids aged zero to five whose parents were on drugs, and that was Child Haven. The kids went there every day until they aged out of the system.

Once we founded DADS, and Child Haven found out about what we were trying to do, they became super supportive of us and our ministry. At Christmas time, they would give us vanloads of toys to give to our fathers, and wrote donation checks for DADS and just generally were extremely generous. When the COVID-19 pandemic hit, they went through layoffs and their support dried up for a while.

After a few years, I thought we had heard the last of them until I received that call out of nowhere, shortly after we had the bookshelves built, from someone with the agency. They wanted to know if we would like some books. Books!

Our library shelves are full now, and I never had to ask for anything. The Lord brought me what we needed.

The Needs of the Community

What we are doing at DADS these days is so much bigger than me, and so much bigger even than Seattle. The Lord told me twenty-plus years ago, "Marvin, there should be something like DADS in every major metropolitan city in this country." And I believe that I'm witnessing the first step of that future becoming a reality.

I'm seeing the changed lives of men every day. I have stories and stories on top of stories of men who come through our doors who are now being responsible fathers. And it's because somebody's taking the time to talk about the dynamics of fatherhood and the dynamics of their past and their own fatherhood journeys.

The majority of us have stories of what led us astray and we never think to connect them to our own fathers and families. I want to be that one who puts those stories together for the men we serve, so then they can grab a hold of their own lives and navigate their own families toward a positive outcome. That's both rewarding and impactful to all of us.

We have guys who come through our doors who are angry, and nobody has ever asked, "Why are you angry?" or said, "What led you to become angry—maybe we need to look at that." I'm not a therapist but I can pull on that string and once they start talking, say, "Maybe you need to go see a therapist to help you navigate that."

Having someone ask about them personally, someone who has been through the same struggles, changes everything in a lot of ways for these men. Up to this point, they've felt like they're fighting the whole world on their own. But now they know there's a community of men out there who want to do right by their kids and their families, just like they do. It's a community they didn't even know existed—and now they're a part of it! We aren't *creating* this community; we are giving it a place. We just give the men the opportunity to sit down and be heard and sometimes that's all it takes.

Learning to Trust God's Provision

Recognizing that all we need comes from God, not our own efforts, is a lifelong lesson. It's a journey, just like fatherhood is a journey, and one that DADS has been on since its inception, as have I, personally.

I remember being in treatment and praying this prayer: "God, help me put my family back together again." I was new in my faith walk and I was receiving treatment in a ninety-day program and living in a little apartment inside of a building that was full of recovering addicts. I had a room to myself and it was kind of like my first little place that I had on my own. During this time, I found a job at an insurance company where I opened up envelopes and separated the cash from the checks. I was in the midst of my addiction at that time, and I was still using, and so that job scared me to death. It scared me because I saw myself going to the penitentiary. I could easily have taken the cash and put it in my pocket and left.

I thought about that for days. It would have been so easy. The temptations were certainly there. I'd imagine going somewhere nice and leaving this job behind—maybe even taking a girl with me—but I knew that was the devil pulling me, trying to get me to do something that would set me back. So, I quit the job. Even though I wasn't strong enough to quit using at that time, I was strong enough to walk away from the temptation to steal. I knew I couldn't be trusted for long around all that cash and God gave me the wisdom and strength to remove myself from that situation.

I didn't feel right, though, about how I ended things with that job, and my family needed me to keep working. That was when, with God's help, I finally got myself clean. After I got out of rehab, I went back to the hiring agency and talked to the executive director. I told him "Listen, I know I didn't leave you in the right way, but I'm asking you for another opportunity." I told him that I had been addicted to crack and that I had left for the good of the company and my own integrity. After hearing my story, he was willing to me another chance.

He said, "Okay, I can try you again. I appreciate you coming and telling me this and, yeah, I'll give you another opportunity." Whew. God was teaching me the blessings of obedience, as well as to trust in His provision.

The new job was working for Goodwill, opening up and running a donation station in Totem Lake. A donation station is really just a little hut, a twenty-foot container, and some firewood. As the one running the station, my job was to make sure the container was filled up for when, every three days, the truck would come pick that container up and drop another one. I was so happy to have this opportunity because, at this time, I was still trying to get my kids back home. I was trying to be a good husband and father, and this was at the very beginning stages of all of that.

So, I got up every day and went to Totem Lake to work my little hut. I was staying clean, and Jeanett was in treatment. It felt like we were making progress. I could start to see a new life for us taking shape in my mind.

Once Jeanett got out of treatment, she started catching the bus out to Totem Lake and she'd come sit with me, and that was the beginning stages of our walk with the Lord. When things were slow at the donation station, I would sit and read my Bible, and it became a habit. I was looking at all the good stuff that was happening for me in my life, and I thought, *Lord, if I just trust You for everything like I trusted the devil for everything when I was living the way I was living, then I can't go wrong.* That was just the simple mathematics I put together in my own mind. So, I would read the Old Testament, see how God worked in the lives of people in its pages, and then I would look at things that would happen to me—and it felt like providence.

Someone would pull up and give me five dollars to get some coffee. People would drive up and say, "Do you have a family?" and I'd say yes and they'd respond, "Well go take this to your family." Repeatedly, people kept showing up for me and I felt like the Lord was covering me, because my family needed it.

During this time, Jeanett found a job as well and we were finally able to bring our children home. We moved out of our clean and sober housing and found a house to stay in. We were doing it. We were building a life for our kids. I just watched the way the Lord was manifesting himself in my life and I was overwhelmed. I had decided to trust this God that people were talking about with everything I had, and He took care of my family in ways I couldn't have imagined. (If you'd like to read more about this part of my story, I tell it in more detail in my first book, *Becoming DADS: A Mission to Restore Absent Fathers*.)

My circumstances radically and fundamentally changed because I put my life in God's hands, and He transformed it. When Jeanett and I started DADS, I remember hearing the voice of the Lord: **"Don't go looking for anything because what you need, I'll bring it to your door."** Well, it's twenty-six years later and He's still doing the same thing.

And now, when God says, "Don't ask for anything; I'll bring you what you need," I can see that it's not my personal needs being met. It's the needs of the *community*, because the needs of the people are the needs of this ministry.

PASS IT ON

God's provision comes "according to the riches of His glory in Christ Jesus," indicating that it is abundant and rooted in the relationship with Christ. Because He is unlimited in all His capacities, so is His provision for our lives.

> "And my God will meet all your needs according to the riches of his glory in Christ Jesus."
> (Philippians 4:19)

CHAPTER 13

Expanding the Vision of DADS

When we first started DADS, one thing became abundantly clear: there should be an organization like this in every urban center in the country. The need is far too great, and the number of men struggling to find their footing in fatherhood is far too high to be ignored. Every time I travel to a new city, I make it a habit to rent a car, drive downtown, and look for the places where men gather around burning barrels to keep warm. These are men who are often discarded by society, yet many of them are fathers. As I stand there counting heads, and imagining how many fatherless children they might account for, I ask myself, "Who is reaching out to these men? Who is guiding them through the complex waters of fatherhood?" The answer is often disheartening—no one. And that must change.

A Hands-On Approach to Fatherhood Programs

There are countless programs that encourage fatherhood in a general sense—show up, participate in activities, spend time with your children. But what about the men who don't even know where to start? What about the ones whose own fathers were absent? Many of these programs provide a framework but fail to walk step by step with these men through their highs and lows. At DADS, we believe in being active participants in the lives of these fathers, helping them correct mindsets and behaviors that have kept them from being the parents their children need. This requires more than just advice—it requires mentorship, accountability, and genuine connection.

Society often turns its back on men who have battled addiction or served time in prison. They are viewed as too far gone, as individuals who are beyond redemption. But we see them differently. These men represent an opportunity—a chance to rewrite not only their own stories but the stories of their children and future generations. By creating an environment where they feel part of a supportive community, we can help them reintegrate into society, reestablish relationships with their children, and ultimately prevent the cycle of incarceration from continuing.

I am not convinced that enough is being done in this space, and I am determined to keep working to change that. The stigma surrounding these men needs to be replaced with support, mentorship, and resources that can help them break free from their past and build a future centered on faith, fatherhood, and responsibility.

Collaboration and Growth

I'm incredibly encouraged about the future of DADS and the work we can do not just at home here in Seattle, but eventually across the nation. Part of the reason for that enthusiasm is a young man I met three, maybe four, years ago in Portland. He'd been involved in gang violence, incarceration, all of that, but he'd made a real change in his life and wanted to give back. I remember he was around fifteen years younger than me, but he thought like I did—he cared about people, really cared. He told me he'd bought a small duplex and was using one unit to house a family, while the other served as transitional housing for men coming out of prison. I thought, "Hey, let me help you with that. Let me mentor you. I've walked that path, too."

So, he and his wife came to Seattle, and we spent time together. I showed him around and introduced him to people and programs. Eventually, we started meeting up in Bend, Oregon, at a place we called "The Weekend." He had connections in Portland, and I had connections in Seattle, so we'd use those weekends to share what was working and support each other. It has been amazing to watch his progress—he's done so much.

This young man started working with men coming out of prison, breaking up gang conflicts, and creating a positive shift in their lives. I saw this firsthand during a retreat I led at the Murdock Charitable Trust Facility in Vancouver, Washington a while ago. I was down there with our board, strengthening relationships and setting goals, and I caught up with him to see how things were going. He showed me how his work had expanded and then said something that really struck me: "Marvin, the one thing I'm missing is the father component. I can work with these guys all day, but without a father figure in their lives, we're just going to keep seeing these cycles repeat."

That's when we talked about partnering. He was planning to take his team to Baltimore to learn gang prevention techniques, and after that, we agreed our teams would start collaborating. We took some of our team to Portland to train with him and his people, and he sent some of his folks to Seattle. We wanted them to see how we handle relationships with child support services, the Department of Social and Health Services, and the courts—how we help men navigate these systems.

One day, as I was watching all these men coming out of prison and showing up at his office, I asked him, "How many of these guys are fathers?"

He said, "Ninety percent."

Imagine the impact we could have if we could reach that 90 percent and help them reconnect with their children. That's our opportunity!

This partnership sparked a vision for what we call the "I-5 Corridor" project. Michael, my Portland partner, said, "Marvin, think about it this way: I-5 runs from Canada to Mexico. We used to get on I-5 to do wrong—now let's use it for good. Let's turn it into a pathway for fathers getting out of prison to reunite with their kids." So, we're working to make that happen, to spread this work up and down the I-5 Corridor.

I also see this work expanding nationally. We've got partners in Tulsa, Oklahoma, and Los Angeles. One of our team, Maria, speaks fluent Spanish, and she has translated some of our materials for the Hispanic community. It opened a door. Now, Hispanic fathers who might have struggled with language barriers can understand and benefit from our resources. This idea, that every urban center in this country could have a program like ours, is something I feel was meant to happen.

Just recently, I traveled to three different correctional institutions to share my story and speak directly to incarcerated men. I firmly believe that if men learn how to reconnect with their children, they are far less likely to return to prison. More importantly, if they shift their focus from simply avoiding incarceration to actively preventing their children from walking the same path, entire family trees can be transformed.

God is creating opportunities for us to beta-test this concept in new places. We are challenging these men to think beyond their own circumstances and to envision a better future for their children. If we can equip them with the tools they need to reconnect and rebuild, we can dramatically reduce recidivism and break generational cycles of broken homes and absent fathers.

A Call to Action

Ten years ago, I read an article from the UK that has stayed with me ever since. It spoke about "man deserts"—entire communities where there are no men leading households. This is not just an American issue; it is a global crisis. The same problem exists in the UK, Russia, and in many other parts of the world. Fatherlessness is one of the most pressing social issues of our time, and the work we are doing through DADS is not just important—it is essential.

There is a big future in this work, but it's not a path I would recommend lightly. If you want to get involved, you must have a heart for this work, you must be ready to ride the rollercoaster that comes with it. It is not an easy road, but it is a necessary one. The good news is that DADS has the tools, resources, and community to support those who are willing to take up the mantle. We are committed to walking with those who join us, mentoring them, and equipping them with the knowledge and strategies that have proven effective.

This is not a casual commitment. It requires deep reflection, a willingness to learn, and an understanding that this work is about changing the culture of the world as we know it. But if you are ready, we are here to walk with you.

The vision for DADS is not just about expanding an organization—it is about changing lives, restoring families, and ultimately shifting the course of entire communities. We are already seeing the impact, but there is so much more to be done. If you believe in this mission, if you see the need in your own community, and if you feel called to make a difference, now is the time to step forward.

This is not just my vision—it is a collective mission that requires all of us. Fatherlessness will not disappear on its own. It takes intentional effort, unwavering faith, and a willingness to invest in the lives of men who have been overlooked for far too long.

Together, we can mend what has been broken. Together, we can change the world.

PASS IT ON

A request for blessing and expansion is not selfish but rooted in a desire for God's favor. As His children, beloved by Him, we can confidently seek God's blessing with the intent to honor Him and further His Kingdom.

> *And Jabez called out to the God of Israel,*
> *"If only You would bless me and enlarge my territory!*
> *May Your hand be with me and keep me from*
> *harm, so that I will be free from pain."*
> *And God granted the request of Jabez.*
> (1 Chronicles 4:10)

Acknowledgments

To my beloved wife, Jeanett Charles—

Wife, co-founder, and unwavering partner in both life and ministry. Your strength, faith, and relentless love have been the foundation of this work. Divine Alternatives for Dads Services would not exist without your vision, your sacrifice, and your steadfast belief in this mission. I could not have done this without you. Together, we have built more than an organization—we have built a legacy.

To my bonus mother, Emma Cotton—

In a time of deep personal loss, you became a constant source of love and strength. Since the passing of my adoptive mother and my maternal mother, your steadfast support has been a blessing I will forever cherish.

To my children and grandchildren—

You are the reason and the reward. May the legacy of fatherfulness, of presence, of love, and of purpose—be carried through your lives and into the generations yet to come. You are the continuation of this dream.

ACKNOWLEDGMENTS

To my editor, Timothy Lawrence—the proud son of Doug and Arlyn Lawrence, and now a proud new father himself—

Working alongside you on this project has been both an honor and a joy. Your attention to detail, your heartfelt engagement with the message, and your commitment to excellence have not only shaped this book but have helped steward a vision that will impact generations. Thank you for your partnership, your professionalism, and your heart.

To Arlyn Lawrence—Founder, President, Editor-in-Chief—and the entire team at Inspira Literary Solutions—

It has been my privilege to entrust five projects into your capable hands. Your motto, *"From idea-in-head to book-in-hand, our aim at Inspira Literary Solutions is to be a publishing resource and support to anyone with a manuscript, message, or mission they want to get into print,"* has not simply been a promise—it has been my lived experience, every step of the way. Through your guidance, encouragement, and expertise, you have helped ensure that the message of hope, healing, and fatherfulness reaches far beyond these pages. I am deeply grateful for your role in building a legacy that I pray will bless countless fathers, families, and communities for generations to come.

About the Author

Marvin Charles is the founder and executive director of Divine Alternatives for Dads Services. For over thirty years, he has been effectively helping men reclaim their positive role as the fathers their children need. Marvin's own powerful story of separation and reunification with his family, parents, and children, fueled his passion for ministry, gave him experience, and earned the trust of other men to be their mentor and advisor.

Marvin is also an emerging national leader in creating stronger fathers and healthier families. He travels across the U.S. to speak about empowering fathers, to learn from other national leaders, and to share his successes with other organizations planning to implement fatherhood programs.

Marvin is the author of *Becoming Dads: A Mission to Restore Absent Fathers*, which chronicles his life and the beginnings of DADS. He is also the author of the *Becoming DADS Innovative Fatherhood Curriculum*, with Dr. George R. Williams, PhD, and of the *Doing DADS: Intake and Support Manual* with his wife, Jeanett Charles. Marvin is an ordained minister and his extraordinary effectiveness comes from his ability to see through the pain and threats of those he counsels to the powerful change possible by embracing a living God and larger purpose.

Marvin and Jeanett live and serve in Seattle, Washington. They have eight children and a growing number of grandchildren in whom they take great delight.

www.aboutdads.org

Other Books and Resources by Marvin Charles and D.A.D.S.

Marvin Charles' first book, *Becoming DADS: A Mission to Restore Absent Fathers*, combines heart-wrenching realities with vital information that graphically portrays the problem of fatherlessness in our society. *Becoming DADS* lays out practical strategies for restoring absentee fathers to their families and helping them develop the skills they need to be engaged, effective dads.

ISBN 978-0-9976009-0-2

The *Becoming DADS Innovative Fatherhood Curriculum*, by Marvin Charles and George Williams, Ph.D., is designed to educate and empower men in challenging situations to take the needed responsibility and action so their children can thrive and be successful. With participant and facilitator guides, this acclaimed curriculum is ideal for group use or one-on-one mentoring with men who want to grow in their fathering skills.

ISBN 978-1-952943-98-0

The *Doing DADS Intake and Resource Manual*, by Marvin and Jeanett Charles, is the quintessential resource for organizations desiring to establish their own "D.A.D.S." services. This is the manual that puts into one volume the vision, strategy, and practical steps to starting and running a D.A.D.S. ministry—a helping community of caring friends working together to reunite families. Here you'll find information and advice for getting started, building your team, and setting up your office and client services.

ISBN 978-1-952943-99-7

Marvin Charles' books and curricular resources are available on *Amazon.com*, *BarnesandNoble.com* or anywhere books are sold. For bulk discounts, inquire directly through the contact page at *About Dads.org*.

ISBN 978-1-952943-12-6